Centripetal and Centrifugal
Structures in Biblical Poetry

*THE SOCIETY OF BIBLICAL LITERATURE*
# MONOGRAPH SERIES

Adela Yarbro Collins, Editor
E.F. Campbell, Associate Editor

Number 39
CENTRIPETAL AND CENTRIFUGAL
STRUCTURES IN BIBLICAL POETRY

by
Daniel Grossberg

Daniel Grossberg

# CENTRIPETAL AND CENTRIFUGAL STRUCTURES IN BIBLICAL POETRY

Scholars Press
Atlanta, Georgia

# CENTRIPETAL AND CENTRIFUGAL STRUCTURES IN BIBLICAL POETRY

by
Daniel Grossberg

©1989
The Society of Biblical Literature

**Library of Congress Cataloging in Publication Data**

Grossberg, Daniel
Centripetal and centrifugal structures in Biblical
poetry.
    (The Society of Biblical Literature monograph
series ; no. 39)
    Bibliography: p.
1. Bible.  O.T. Psalms CXX-CXXXIV--Language, style.
2. Bible.  O.T.  Song of Solomon--Language, style.
3. Bible.  O.T.  Lamentations--Language, style.
4. Hebrew poetry, Biblical. I. Title. II. Series.
BS1445.S6G76 1989  223'.066          89-10194
ISBN 1-55540-360-3  (alk. paper)
ISBN 1-55540-361-1  (pbk. : alk. paper)

Printed in the United States of America
on acid-free paper

To
my wife Millie
and our children
Penina, Yaffa Shira and Sharona

# CONTENTS

Contents

# PREFACE

Biblical poetry has been a strong concern of mine for many years. Various stages in the production of this book attest to that abiding interest. I acknowledge also the many individuals over the several years who have influenced the outcome of this volume.

Parts of Chapter 2 appeared under the title, "A Centrifugal Structure in Biblical Poetry" in *Semiotica* in 1986. In an abbreviated and more primitive form, I presented aspects of chapters 1 and 3 to my colleagues in the Biblical Hebrew Poetry Section of the Society of Biblical Literature Annual Meetings of 1987 and 1988. I am grateful to the researchers who shared their reactions with me. Their suggestions enhanced this work.

I use this occasion also to thank Professor Cyrus H. Gordon who introduced me to the excitement in biblical, Hebrew and Semitic studies.

I express particular thanks to Professor Edward F. Campbell Jr., Associate Editor of the Society of Biblical Literature Monograph Series. I fully appreciate his careful reading of the MS, his incisive comments and his warm encouragement.

I acknowledge above all my indebtedness to my wife and children to whom I dedicate this book.

Abbreviations in this work follow the Society of Biblical Literature Instructions.

The University at Albany
January, 1989

# INTRODUCTION

## *The Aim of This Study of Biblical Poetry*

The Songs of Ascents (Pss 120-134), Song of Songs and Lamentations share the distinction of being written entirely in poetry. However we define poetry and distinguish it from prose, these three biblical works fit squarely within the poetic grouping. In the course of this study characteristics of biblical poetry will arise.

The insistence on the poetic quality of these works at the outset of this study suggests some fundamental principles of my work. My approach to the three poetic compositions is decidedly synchronic.[1] I direct my attention to constituent units of the compositions. In my analysis of each poem, I isolate for scrutiny sounds, words, phrases and sentences as well as suprasentential segments, up to the poem as a whole. I discern a distinct tension among and between the parts and the whole in the structural design of each poem. The essence of the present investigation is an analysis of the poetic composition of The Songs of Ascents, Song of Songs and Lamentations in terms of the particular structural tensions at work in each.

Modern critical scholarship has examined the Songs of Ascents as it has studied the full range of psalms. The structure and style of the psalms have also been the object of analyses. The investigators, however, have paid but scanty attention to Pss 120-134 as a group and a unity. Beyond acknowledging the common superscription and commenting *en passant* on the brevity of these psalms and the degree of repetition within

---

[1] In the present study, the Masoretic text (MT), the received Hebrew text, is the object of examination; concern with textual variants is not. I touch upon the time and place of composition of Lamentations and Songs of Ascents; I comment in passing on the historical situation of their composition; and I broach the subject of authorship in Lamentations. These historically oriented issues, however, are not the aim of this volume. Similarly, earlier sources and layers that may have been incorporated into the works under consideration are not within the purview of this study. It is my contention that there are deliberate and elaborate rhetorical designs discernible in the MT. Whose hand is responsible for these designs is immaterial in this investigation. For convenience, I refer to that deliberate hand as "the poet" or "the artist" or some analogous term.

them, there has been little written about the Songs of Ascents as a whole. I am pleased to recognize the work of Cuthbert C. Keet[2] and Evode Beaucamp[3] as exceptions to this generalization.

Song of Songs differs from Songs of Ascents and Lamentations in that the structure of the Song has been the subject of much study.[4] Aside from Francis S. Landy[5] and Michael V. Fox,[6] two welcome recent works, the numerous studies, by and large, attempted to impose too elaborate a design or designs on the Songs, or conversely, looked upon Canticles as an indiscriminate aggregate of poetic pieces lacking literary integrity. Advocates of constricting patterns and advocates of the disunity theory of Song of Songs alike fail to see the essential structural composition of the Song of Songs.

The alphabetic acrostic arrangements of chaps. 1-4 of Lamentations constitute a major organizing principle in the book. This external ordering of the verses is so conspicuous a basis for arrangement that it has been taken as the only basis. Statements like the following are not unusual: "Each verse. . .is. . .linked to the other members of the alphabetic group *only* by virtue of the acrostic."[7] This arrangement of verses has given rise to the notion that the sequence of verses in Lamentations is wholly artificial and mechanical. The view that the book consists of five *independent* poems dealing with a common theme reinforced the conception that Lamentations is an anthology of elegies with no inner progress within the individual poems or among them, within the entire book. Hermann Gunkel identified chaps. 1, 2, and 4 mainly as funeral songs, chap. 3 primarily as an individual lament, and chap. 5 as a communal lament.[8] Discussions of the literary form of the work

[2] C. C. Keet, *A Study of the Psalms of Ascents: A critical and exegetical commentary upon Psalms cxx to cxxxiv* (London: Mitre Press, 1969).

[3] E. Beaucamp, "L'unité du Recueil des Montées: Psaumes 120-134," *Liber annuus Studium Biblicum Franciscanum* 29 (1979) 73-90.

[4] See M. H. Pope, *Song of Songs: A New Translation with Introduction and Commentary* (AB 7C [Garden City, N.Y.: Doubleday, 1977] 40-50) for a discussion of the literary integrity of Song of Songs and bibliography.

[5] F. Landy, *Paradoxes of Paradise: Identity and Difference in the Song of Songs* (Sheffield: Almond Press, 1983).

[6] M. V. Fox, *The Song of Songs and Ancient Egyptian Love Songs* (Madison and London: University of Wisconsin Press, 1985).

[7] G. M. Schramm, "Poetic Patterning in Biblical Hebrew" In *Michigan Oriental Studies in Honor of George G. Cameron*, ed. L. L. Orlin (Ann Arbor: University of Michigan, 1976) 178. The italics are mine.

[8] H. Gunkel, *Einleitung in die Psalmen* (Gottingen: Vandenhoeck und Ruprecht, 1933).

have concentrated on the *qīnāh* meter with reference to the acrostic style. Attention to the inner structure has been minimal but worthy of recognition: Albert Condamin[9] and William Shea[10] study the book as a whole and discern in it symmetrical patterns of structure. Alan Mintz also rises above the single line and traces narrative and dramatic development of the theme.[11]

In the wider realm of the generic study of Hebrew poetry, Donald Broadribb concluded in 1972 that, historically, attention to parallelism and meter has dominated the field, with strophic concerns also prominent.[12] The studies, for the most part, focus on one aspect of Hebrew poetry without treating the poem globally and without observing the interaction of the poetic elements. Within the 1980s some significant studies of Hebrew poetry have appeared. Although interest and value attach to these investigations, the concentration of the discourses on Hebrew poetry has not changed substantially. I comment briefly on four of these recent valuable studies:

James L. Kugel brought his vast knowledge of literary criticism to bear on Hebrew poetry in *The Idea of Biblical Poetry: Parallelism and Its History*.[13] His work has affected the way the reader of the Bible understands parallelism. The reader no longer views parallelism as a repetition of an idea for rhetorical purposes as Abraham Ibn Ezra (1089-1164) asserted.[14] Kugel points to the parallelistic reiteration as a "going one better"; a restatement with a nuance—an implicit "and what's more!" However perceptive Kugel's analysis is, it treats but one aspect of poetry, an important one, but only one, nevertheless. Adele Berlin, with careful scholarship and pedagogical clarity, broadens the scope of the study of parallelism. *The Dynamics of Biblical Parallelism* examines various aspects of parallelism: grammatical, lexical and semantic, and phonological.[15] Berlin

---

[9] A. Condamin, "Symmetrical Repetitions in *Lamentations* Chapters I and II." *JTS* 7 (1906) 137-40.

[10] W. H. Shea, "The *qīnāh* Structure of the Book of Lamentations," *Bib* 60 (1979) 103-7.

[11] A. Mintz, "The Rhetoric of Lamentations and the Representation of Catastrophe," *Prooftexts* 2 (1982) 1-17 and *Ḥurban: Responses to Catastrophe in Hebrew Literature* (New York: Columbia University Press, 1984).

[12] D. Broadribb, "A Historical Review of Studies of Hebrew Poetry," *Abr-N* 13 (1972) 66-87.

[13] J. L. Kugel, *The Idea of Biblical Poetry* (New Haven and London: Yale University Press, 1981).

[14] Abraham Ibn Ezra on Num 21:17; 23:7; Deut 32:7 and on other parallelistic repetitions in biblical poetry, see *Rabbinic Bible* (*Miqrā'ōt Gĕdōlōt*).

[15] A. Berlin, *The Dynamics of Biblical Parallelism* (Bloomington: Indiana University Press, 1985).

shows that the poetic text displays an interplay of the aspects creating a density and multivalence. *The Dynamics of Biblical Parallelism* is a partial corrective to the common studies of Hebrew poetry. Berlin aims in the direction of a total, overall understanding. Berlin, however, does not analyze units above the parallel couplet. If, indeed, parallelism is the "constructive principle on which a poem is built" as Berlin claims,[16] she does not treat the significant part of the poem that is built on the greater parallelisms of the text, e.g., its open and close, its distant echoes, the dynamic shifting of its elements, etc.

Robert Alter's work[17] differs from Kugel's and Berlin's. Whereas theirs is an abstraction of a technique, an identification of a principle, *The Art of Biblical Poetry* is an analysis of sample texts. With extraordinary literary sense, Alter explicates biblical poems with his eye on the larger unit that is comprised of smaller ones. Intensification is a significant relationship of the larger to the smaller. Alter demonstrates a "powerful sense of process" in series of poetic lines.[18] *The Art of Biblical Poetry* is most different from *The Idea of Biblical Poetry* and the *Dynamics of Biblical Parallelism* in its transferability. Alter's readings, and Kugel's and Berlin's too, are insightful. But the degree to which readers can learn from Alter's book and apply his approach to other texts is limited. The limitation is as great as is the difference between the reader's artistic sensitivity and the artistic sensitivity of Robert Alter.

Harold Fisch also addresses biblical poetry as literary text in *Poetry With A Purpose: Biblical Poetics and Interpretation.*[19] Fisch analyzes several texts with an eye on the degree of similarity of each to a familiar literary form or extrabiblical genre. The similarity, Fisch argues, is always elusive and incomplete. As the Bible develops a likeness to an aesthetic form, it also undermines the likeness. Fisch sees this subversion as the essence of the biblical poetics. Scripture cannot be apprehended solely by literary/aesthetic means. Greater value would obtain if Fisch were to have identified at the outset the familiar form(s) the Bible adheres to and the nature of the subversion(s) it effects. Otherwise, the biblical poetics and interpretation Fisch purports to present are as varied as the texts he approaches.

In the chapters that follow, I examine structural features on

---

[16] Berlin, *Dynamics*, 6.
[17] R. Alter, *The Art of Biblical Poetry* (New York: Basic Books, 1985).
[18] Alter, *Poetry*, 36.
[19] H. Fisch, *Poetry With a Purpose* (Bloomington: Indiana University Press, 1988) 36.

the level of the individual line and above it. I direct my atten-
tion to the dynamic interplay among the several features of the
poems as reflective of the artistic tension inherent in all poetry.

## Categories and Terminology

The field upon which poetry plays is the continuum joining
the extreme of unity to the extreme of variety. Poetry is a series
of discrete units upon the field and at the same time it is also the
total field. There are factors operating in every poetic text that
lend varying degrees of connectedness to the discrete units of
the work. The predominant formal feature of the poem is its
articulation of these distinct units into a series of organized parts
that are both distinct from and related to each other and that
together form a unified whole. The reader fully appreciates the
poetic work in terms of the cumulative effect of the parts which
create the total artistic construction. The degree of unity and
wholeness, however, is not constant. The complexity and dy-
namic character of poetry derive from the tension and balance
of the parts with each other and with the whole.

Some poetic texts tend to highlight the unity of the whole;
others tend toward a dominant emphasis on the parts. Poetic
works, therefore, can be typed by determining the location of
their compositional structuring on a centripetal/centrifugal
continuum.[20]

At the centripetal extreme are those poetic works marked by
a prevailing uniform structure and tight pattern; at the
centrifugal extreme are those works with disparate figures and a
predominantly loose composition. In the former, the parts
unify, centralize and contribute to the coherence of the whole.
The second type stresses detail for its own sake, tends away from
centralization and thus evidences an atomistic structure. The
effect of the complete text of this latter type is more of a loose
aggregate with the parts perceived in succession, than of an in-
tegrated assemblage featuring a simultaneity.

Arthur Mizener identifies the loose structural tendency in
Yeats's art with "romantic" poetry. He describes Yeats's poetry
as "full of enthusiastic and crotchety extremes which are forever
on the verge of destroying its coherence of statement or its
unity of style. It knows neither decorum of idea . . . nor deco-

---

[20] I owe the category descriptions "centripetal" and "centrifugal" and much of
their descriptions to E. Stankiewicz ("Centripetal and Centrifugal Structures in Po-
etry," *Semiotica* 38 [1982] 217-42).

rum of vocabulary."[21]

On the other hand, a centripetal structure is one that is marked by "tension." I use this term as defined by Edward A. Bloom,

> . . .to refer to the meaningful complexity, to the interactions between the parts and the whole, between one part and another, between the concrete and the abstract, between one mood and another, which make a poem "work within itself" and be worthy of careful rereading and analysis.[22]

The twofold typology—centripetal/centrifugal—is not an absolute dichotomy. Historical periods, literary genres and individual works exhibit structural tendencies of both types. Particular interest attaches to composites of complicated and interrelated characteristics of the two tendencies at work within one corpus. The strength of the contrasting forces is not equal. Each work finds its balance at a different place on the centripetal/centrifugal scale.

Modern lyrical poetry displays a strong penchant for the centrifugal structure. Stankiewicz briefly sketches the forerunners of this modern predilection beginning with Tasso and his followers in the 16th century. The aesthetic program of the Tassists, asserts Stankiewicz, showed the following characteristics (among others) of the centrifugal type of structure: the loose connection of heterogeneous parts, the lack of strong terminal closure, and the accumulation of new and unusual metaphors.[23]

The Baroque added "the *concetto*, i.e., the use of daring metaphors (including oxymora) that were scattered through the text in unpredictable combinations, like gems in an icon, and that were meant to dazzle the reader."[24]

The trend toward open, centrifugal forms rose again in the romantic reaction to classical poetry and reached its peak in the modern period especially in symbolist poetry.

Stankiewicz contrasts the centrifugal forms of modernism with the "classical" centripetal texts that display an ordered and goal-directed movement and completeness. The centripetal

---

[21] A. Mizener, "The Romanticism of W. B. Yeats," *The Southern Review* 7 (1942) 622.

[22] E. A. Bloom, C. H. Philbrick, and E. H. Blistein, *The Order of Poetry: An Introduction* (New York: Odyssey Pres, 1961) 167.

[23] Stankiewicz, "Centripetal," 224.

[24] Ibid.

tendency features a unified whole marked by formal figures of closure, e.g., refrains and strong final close. These devices delineate the composition and integrate the disparate parts into a self-contained and meaningful whole.

## Three Biblical Poetic Corpora and Their Compositional Form

Neither the modern nor the medieval period was the first to develop a compositional form that manifested a predominant tendency toward the centrifugal extreme or the centripetal extreme. Examples of these tendencies are also to be found in antiquity.

Examples of various structural types located at various points along the centripetal/centrifugal continuum appear in the Hebrew Scriptures. The Songs of Ascents are fifteen consecutive psalms (Pss 120-134) within the Psalter. Each of these discrete compositions displays tightening and centralizing features that highlight its unity and autonomy at the expense of the totality of the small collection. Examined together, however, these psalms evidence a tendency toward an organic whole exhibiting a unity. The centripetal extreme and the centrifugal extreme each exerts its countervailing forces on the structural form of the Songs of Ascents.

The Song of Songs exhibits a compositional structure marked by numerous atomizing features which tend toward a dominant emphasis on the parts. The Song maintains an artistic tension between unity and variety, between integrity and detail, by displaying centralizing features that partially offset the disjunctive forces. The compositional tension in Song of Songs finds its resolution near the centrifugal extreme on the centripetal/centrifugal continuum.

Lamentations strikes a balance between the predominance of the whole and the emphasis on the parts with its point of balance somewhere midway on the structural scale. There are at work in Lamentations tighter, more well-defined ties among its parts than is apparent in Canticles or in the Songs of Ascents. At the same time, fragmenting forces exert their influence on the compositional form of Lamentations, causing a dynamic tension here, too, on the centripetal/centrifugal continuum.

## A Partial Catalogue of Centripetal and Centrifugal Features

I present here several of the more prominent stylistic features that affect the compositional form of the Songs of Ascents, Song of Songs and Lamentations. I subtitle this section advisedly. This catalogue is not exhaustive. The qualifying "partial" announces that I do not presume to identify all the centripetal and centrifugal features at work in poetic texts or even at work in the poetic texts discussed in the present study.

The composition of a poem is too flu;id to allow a simple counting, first of the centripetal features and then of the centrifugal features. Cleanth Brooks emphasizes the dynamism inherent in poetic structure in his groping for appropriate analogies:

> The essential structure of a poem . . . resembles that of architecture or painting: it is a pattern of resolved stresses. Or, . . . the structure of a poem resembles that of a ballet or musical composition. It is a pattern of resolutions and balances and harmonizations, developed through a temporal scheme. Or, . . . the structure of a poem resembles that of a play . . . for the very nature of drama is that of something which arrives at its conclusion through conflict—something which builds conflict into its very being.[25]

In the present study, I identify numerous stylistic features in poetry in order to examine their combined effects on compositional form. The mere identification of the features is not my goal: the effects of the features on the structure of the entire work is the aim. The expository nature of this study is necessarily isolating. The power of the poem, on the other hand, is in the concert and symphony of all its elements. Some may be emphasized and some may be subordinated, but their combination and correlation is fundamental. My treatment of them seriatim should in no way be construed as an indication of the manner in which they operate in a poem.

I now proceed to list and briefly describe several of the salient stylistic features appearing in the Songs of Ascents, The Song of Songs, and Lamentations that contribute to the establishment of the respective compositional forms of those works. Examples of each feature will be given in the ensuing chapters.

1. Boundary markers are those features on the most macro level of a text that create a centripetal and centrifugal impetus in the work. Closural devices that delimit a text provide autonomy and form. The clearer the boundary, the greater the apprehensibility of the unit so defined. The delimited text is closed and centripetally oriented. Conversely, the open-ended

---

[25] C. Brooks, *The Well Wrought Urn* (New York: Harcourt, Brace and Co., 1947) 203-04.

text lacks sharp definitions and tends toward centrifugality. Openings, closings, and titles are among the main boundary markers.

2. On the level of the individual words, the poet's lexical choice helps define the structural type of the work. M. A. K. Halliday describes how the particular word selection may be a centripetal force: "A word that is in some way associated with another word in the preceding text, because it is a direct repetition of it, or is in some sense synonymous with it, or tends to occur in the same lexical environment, coheres with that word and so contributes to the texture."[26] In the case of such a lexical choice, the corresponding words form networks of meaning and patterns of sequential relations that run through the text. These networks and patterns constitute a significant centripetal tendency.

3. Repetition in its various forms is the most frequent cohesive device. The reiterated unit is recalled and ipso facto related. The function of the restatement, moreover, may be to identify the boundaries of the totality (inclusio); or to demarcate segments of the work (refrain); or to highlight themes and feature development (parallel pieces, elements recurring in different forms at varying intervals, associative clusters and key words); or to impart a texture (all types). By defining the limits of a work or marking its segments, form and integrality emerge from the disparate parts. The work becomes more easily grasped. When the configuration reflects the theme and content, a potent centripetality is apparent.

4. The figurative use of words also affects the cohesion of a work. The literary metaphor, for example, demands that it be given something other than its usual literal interpretation, thus slowing the progress of the text. The slowing allows for the non-literal interpretation which may open and fragment the text. The loosing of the metaphor from the texture can work against the unity of the work. The metaphor identified in isolation, however, may be related to other metaphors and with them form a set of imagery in the text. In this case, the relations constitute threads that knit the work. The metaphor, by its very nature, also strikes novel correspondences which tie and bind.

5. Syntactic structures, on the sentence level of a work or above the single sentence level, may also exert centripetal and centrifugal forces in a poem. The structural similarity of two or

[26] M. A. K. Halliday and R. Hasan, *Cohesion in English* (London: Longman, 1976) 319.

more sentences associates them and adds to the reticulation within the poem. On a simple but instructive plane, Waldemar Gutwinski gives the following example from a nursery rhyme:

> This little pig went to market;
> This little pig stayed home;
> This little pig ate roast beef;
> This little pig had none.[27]

The analogous sentence structure of each line ties the ditty together even in the absence of conjunctions and connectives. Much biblical synonymous parallelism functions in this way. Contrariwise, disparate sentence structures revealing no syntactic parallelism undermines the tightness. New syntactic locutions can also tie together distant and incongruous semantic domains; if carried to an extreme they can lead to the dissolution of meaning and structure.

6. The phonological level of the text is also a potent unifying force. The recurrence of the same sound ipso facto forms a link. The similarity of sound can closely knit the work. If the sound correspondence reflects a semantic relationship, the two levels combine to create yet a denser weave. The assonance or alliteration by itself suggests a notional correspondence between words that otherwise might not be semantically compared. The denser the internal weave, the greater the centripetal orientation.

7. The poetic form of individual lines marked particularly by the elaborate range of parallelism techniques and metric patterns transcends the single verse and forges bonds with other lines. These bonds may link adjacent lines or series of lines or even widely separated lines or units. Too often, parallelism and meter are seen as functioning exclusively within the couplet or adjacent lines. Parallelism and meter include patterns, and their variations, similarities along with dissimilarities, departures and returns, progressions as well as reviews, all making up the texture of verse. These polarities indicate that parallelism and meter are not features with a solely unidirectional centripetal orientation. General regularity should not hide the occasional disjuncture. Regularity creates anticipation which may be satisfied *or* frustrated.

8. Strophic or stanzaic organization and delineation are chief formal features of poetry. The biblical artist, it appears,

---

[27] W. Gutwinski, *Cohesion in Literary Texts: A Study of Some Grammatical and Lexical Feature of English Discourse* (The Hague and Paris: Mouton, 1976) 76.

was not constrained to create uniformly structured or regularly recurring subunits of the entirety. The ancient poet based subunits primarily on content and frequently complemented them by formal markers. The more obvious formal markers are refrains, initial letters (in acrostics), introductory formulae and changes of speaker. These features are not always present. The lack of regularity and the absence of one or several of the features exert an atomizing force. When stanzaic and strophic division markers *are* present, they perform a centralizing function; they help the reader grasp the poem globally.

9. The plot and argument of a literary work weave the parts into a fabric. Conversely, the suppression of a narrative sequence works against the apprehension of the creation in its dramatic integrality. The tension and balance in a poem obtain when the forces toward linear development are counterpoised by features that highlight the parts. The complete lack of "story line" is an invitation to fragmentation. To prevent this, the artist brings unifying forces to bear on the text to rescue it from extreme disjunction.

10. Extratextual references in a literary piece have an ambivalent effect regarding cohesion. A text may make reference explicitly or otherwise to something in another text. For example, an item in one of the psalms may refer to something very specific in another psalm or another part of the Bible. The referent, consequently, relates to the text at hand in a special way. On one level, the allusion breaks the closed nature of the primary text and expands that text, adding diversity of content, style, etc. The reference introduces an openness to the composition. On another plane, by invoking an external referent, the allusion provides an additional source for the understanding and appreciation of the primary text. The extratextual allusion may be the common link that joins two discrete items that only now may be grasped.

11. Historicity can similarly be a force for the tightness or the looseness of a poetic text. An historic referential quality may serve to anchor a fluctuating, open-ended text in an objectifiable setting. At the same time, elements of a realistic record of events may complicate the text at hand by the introduction of alien, obfuscating objective data into a lyrical artistic system. This mingling of historical and lyrical genres may thus open the text and contribute to the centrifugal movement.

12. Shifts of perspective and speaker are also two-directional forces. They may loosen the text by their multiplying of the

frames of reference. They may replace the single tone, speaker and vantage point which serve to concentrate a literary work. The shifts may thus change the focus and expand the range of the text. Paradoxically, the new multivalence resulting from perspectival shifts and shifts of grammatical person may impart a sense of wholeness also. Each shift is an additional small piece of stone producing the patterns in the poem's mosaic. Moreover, the shift may formally signal a subdivision of the text which gives delineation and hence centripetality to the whole.

13. Antithesis and merism both influence structural design. Antithesis serves to create a contrast of thought while merism creates a unity of thought. They both typically use polar word pairs. Antithesis sets one off from the other with a "but on the other hand" understanding. Merism is inclusive: ". . .the unifying nature of merismus counters the polarizing effect of its components. Although, for example, 'going' and 'coming' are opposite in meaning, paradoxically, mention of one arouses expectancy of the other. At the same time the two terms are considered a unity meaning 'whatever you do.'"[28] The antitheses may embrace words, thought, or any poetic unit, within or above the line level.

14. Ambiguity and multiple-meaning serve as either centripetal or centrifugal devices. A polysemous construction, one that can be construed with more than one meaning, may bridge and link two aspects that appear in a poem. On the other hand, the collocation of two seemingly unrelated words in a text may prove disjunctive. The complementary employment of another word or phrase whose various meanings correspond to the "unrelated" words, gathers the threads and weaves them into a tight texture. The interlacing of semantic correspondences is a powerful unifying force. On the other hand, the word of multiple-meaning also brings on momentary vacillation which arrests the progress of the poem centering on the part at the expense of the whole.

15. Chiasm, as one example of several global patterns, is the inverted relationship between the elements of parallel phrases (abc//c'b'a'). These elements may be words, sounds, or grammatical categories within the sentence unit or complete lines or poetic segments above the single-sentence level. They may serve to mark poetic segments, to indicate progression, to show reversal or totality or to feature the pivotal point. All

[28] W. G. E. Watson, *Classical Hebrew Poetry: A Guide to Its Techniques*, JSOTSup 26 (Sheffield: JSOT Press, 1984) 324.

these functions lend unity to the entire poetic text. What is true of chiasm in this respect is true of other formal patterns at work in the poem, e.g., crescendo, diminuendo, etc.

## Outline of This Study

The following chapters focus on the Songs of Ascents, Song of Songs and Lamentations respectively. In each chapter, I identify compositional elements within the particular corpus of biblical poetry studied in that chapter.

I discuss the elements that account for the location of the poems on a structural continuum from dissolution to consolidation. The determination of that location is not merely a tally of pluses and minuses, of centripetal and centrifugal devices. I recognize the dynamism of the poem in the concerted action of opposing features and sometimes in the contrary actions of the same features. I stress that the elements comprising the structural form are in constant tension.

In chapter 1, I treat Pss 120-134. Individually and collectively these psalms are designated Song(s) of Ascents. I examine discrete parts of this cluster and the nature and degree of their articulation. What structural characteristics lead some to grasp the fifteen psalms as an unconnected aggregate and what compositional features account for others understanding the psalms as parts of an integrated assemblage? After reviewing the major interpretations of the ambiguous superscription, *šîr hamma 'ălōt* in order to learn what features are common to the fifteen psalms, I look at the limits of the Songs of Ascents, their "seams" within the fabric of the Psalter. I devote a chief part of chapter 1 to overall explications of several Songs of Ascents with an eye on the interaction of the compositional elements within each psalm that lend it its structural form.

After the analyses of individual psalms, I turn my attention to the small collection as a whole. It is in this section that I present the forces striving toward both wholeness and unity and individuality and separateness, above the level of the discrete psalms. I also present organizational schemas of the totality that knit the parts into a whole. Linguistic peculiarities, extratextuality and narrative development are three rubrics under which I examine the centripetal and centrifugal forces on the level of the totality of the Songs of Ascents.

Chapter 2 centers on the mystery of the structure of the Song of Songs and keys to its unraveling. Peculiar and exotic elements; antiteleological structure; polyphony of voices; abrupt shifts; dazzling images including intersensory figures; poetic ambiguity; architectonic design; repetitions and associations; two sets of parallel pieces, the *waṣfs* and the adjuration; and parallelism formulae are the categories according to which I investigate the interrelated poetic features that give some the impression that the book is an anthology of unconnected love lyrics and others the impression that it is an integrated unity. It becomes clear in this chapter on Song of Songs that many of the same forces for unity are paradoxically forces for disunity as well. The tension is remarkable in the Song and accounts for its puzzling nature.

Chapter 3 treats Lamentations. Five elegies on the single theme of the fall of Jerusalem in 587 B.C.E. comprise the book. Each elegy is, at once, an elaborate, self-contained poetic unit, a grouping of individual elements that strive for prominence in their own right, and an assemblage of poetic units seeking completeness in the totality of the five elegies, creating a unity on the gross level of the book. I examine the following features in chapter 3 with attention to the interplay of their respective loosening and tightening forces: the common theme, the conspicuous and varying acrostic structures of each elegy, the poetic meter characteristic of Lamentations but not unique to it, shifts in speaker and changes in perspective, verbal linking and echoing, the degree of historicity, the peculiar conventional imagery, closural devices, and the various ways of associating and dissociating stanzas. I show that the interaction of these features finds a point of equilibrium near the midpoint on the centripetal/centrifugal continuum.

# CHAPTER 1

## SONGS OF ASCENTS

### THE SUPERSCRIPTION

Psalms 120-134 each carries the superscription *šîr hamma'ălōt*, "Song of Ascents" (Ps 121 *šîr lamma'ălōt*). On the grossest level of structural analysis, features of closure, including the title, the opening and closing lines and other similar boundary markers, define the unity and highlight the autonomy of a text.

Only 24 psalms of the 150 psalms of the MT carry no superscription of any sort. Certainly, therefore, Pss 120-134 are not special merely by having a common title. Nor is 15 a remarkably high number of psalms to bear one particular designation. The superscription of as many as 73 psalms connect those psalms with David. *"mizmōr"* heads 57 psalms; *lamménaṣṣēaḥ* appears in the superscription of 55 psalms; and 30 psalms are entitled *šîr*. What does draw attention to Pss 120-134 is that of all the psalms with headings in the Psalter, it is only the Songs of Ascents which appear consecutively—no Song of Ascents appears in the MT outside of this small collection. None of the other groupings of psalms with like superscriptions are drawn completely together. Despite the consecutive order of the psalms entitled "Songs of Ascents," there is no universally accepted understanding of the designation nor of the nature of the group. The various suggestions and proposals are instructive nevertheless in shedding light on the common elements and characteristics of Pss 120-134 as seen by the proponents of each interpretation.

The LXX translates the term *šîr hamma'ălōt* as *odē tōn anabathmōn*, Jerome as *canticum graduum*, and thus the *KJV* "degrees" and the *RSV* "ascents."

The second part of the term, *ma'ălōt*, appears in 2 Kgs 20:9-11, but it is not clear what was understood by this term. The *NJPS* translates *ma'ălōt* in the 2 Kgs 20 passage as "steps" and includes the note, "A model of a dial with steps has been discovered in Egypt." Pss 120-134 in the *NJPS*, however, are headed by the term "A Song of ascents" with the note, "A term of uncertain meaning."

The following have been the major interpretations of the ambiguous superscription to Pss 120-134:

1. The term "ascents" links the heading to the return from the Babylonian exile. Ezra 7:9 reads, "On the first day of the first month the ascent (*hamma 'ălāh*) from Babylon was started and on the first day of the fifth month he arrived in Jerusalem. . . ." Ezra 7:9 has the singular *ma 'ălāh*, "ascent," whereas our superscription has the plural *ma 'ălōt*, "ascents." Proponents of this interpretation cite Ezra 2 and 8 and explain that the plural refers to more than one journey taken from Babylon to Jerusalem during the reign of Cyrus (Ezra 2) and under Artaxerxes (Ezra 8). Others see the plural reflecting the several caravans. Artur Weiser refers to these psalms as the "Book of Pilgrim Songs" and to each one as "Pilgrim Song." Weiser writes, nevertheless, ". . .but it contains, in fact, only one genuine pilgrim song (Ps 122). . . ."[1] Ps 122 and PS 134 both assume the Temple is still standing and are therefore, inappropriate as referring to the return from Babylon. Further difficulty with this interpretation is the existence of several other psalms in the Psalter that are even more suitable as pilgrim songs and which are not so named (Pss 24, 43, 84, *et al.*).

2. Similar to the former interpretation is the one that takes the *ma 'ălōt*, "ascents," also as pilgrimages to Jerusalem but not after the exile in Babylon. Every male Israelite was enjoined to make pilgrimage to Jerusalem three times a year: at Passover, the Feast of Weeks and *Sukkot*, the Feast of Booths (Deut 16:16; Exod 23:13-17; 34:18-23). Isa 30:29 informs us that singing and rejoicing accompanied these journeys to Jerusalem. This theory holds that the Songs of Ascents preserve several of these pilgrims' songs. Although the verb, *'lh*, "to ascend," is used for a journey to Jerusalem (e.g., Ps 122:4), neither *ma 'ălāh* in the singular nor *ma 'ălōt* in the plural is used of these annual pilgrimages (unless 1 Kgs 12:28, *mē'ălōt*—infinitive construct with privative *mem*—be repointed *ma 'ălōt*).

3. This view, too, relates the superscription to pilgrimages to the Temple in Jerusalem. The word *hamma 'ălōt*, however, is understood as referring to steps in that Temple. Exod 20:26 and 1 Kgs 10:19-20 both employ *ma 'ălōt* in this sense. In two passages, the Mishnah describes the "water drawing" ceremony

[1] A. Weiser, *The Psalms: A Commentary* (Philadelphia: Westminster Press, 1962) 100.

that was performed on the first day of *Sukkot* on the Temple steps. One passage reads, "Fifteen steps led up from within it [Court of the Women] to the Court of the Israelites, corresponding to the fifteen Songs of Ascents in the Psalms, and upon them the Levites used to sing. . . ."[2] Another passage informs us, "And innumerable Levites played on harps, lyres, cymbals and trumpets and musical instruments on the fifteen steps leading down from the Court of the Israelites, corresponding to the fifteen Songs of Ascents in the Psalms."[3] These two citations have been taken as basis for attaching the Songs of Ascents to the songs sung by the Levites on the Temple steps. These Mishnah passages, however, do not indicate that indeed the Songs of Ascents were those sung by the Levites on the steps.

In commenting on the title *šîr hammaʿălôt*, J. F. A. Sawyer writes, "The term means 'The Fifteen', just like 'The Eighteen' (referring to Benedictions). Instead of calling them simply 'The Fifteen', however, the rabbis, with characteristic imagination and originality, called them after the fifteen steps leading up to the temple. . . . Perhaps the best translation of the term would be 'The Songs of the Temple Steps.' "[4]

4. We can distinguish in several of the Songs of Ascents a distinctive poetic structure. A fourth interpretation of the superscription is that of "songs of ascending structure" in which a clause repeats a word or phrase from the preceding clause with an addition or elaboration. A gradual stairlike ascent results as this repetition is continued in subsequent verses. The figure is akin to classical anadiplosis in which a prominent and usually the last word in one phrase is repeated at the beginning of the next. Psalms in this small collection that exhibit this stairlike pattern are Pss 121; 122:2-4; 123:2-4; 124:1-5; 125:2, 3; 126:2, 3; 129:1, 2. These instances of the particular pattern notwithstanding, there remain eight of the fifteen psalms that do not display this pattern. Furthermore, stairlike structures appear in other psalms (e.g., 29) and in Song of Songs (e.g., 1:15; 4:1). Moreover we do not have any evidence of the word *maʿălôt* signifying this technical meaning anywhere else.

5. Another explanation of the heading, also carrying a technical sense, is quoted by David Kimḥe: "Rabbi Saʿadya Gaon, may his name be for a blessing, explained the Songs of Ascents were said with a very great raising of the voice [perhaps in the

---

[2] *Mid.* 2:5.

[3] *Sukk.* 5:4.

[4] J. F. A. Sawyer, "An Analysis of the Context and Meaning of the Psalm-Headings," *Transactions of the Glasgow University Oriental Society* 22 (1967-68) 33.

sense of 'sung in a high key' as rendered by Joshua Baker and
Ernest W. Nicholson[5]. And with each of the songs they used to
raise their voices."[6] This understanding is based on 2 Chron
20:19 in which the Levites are said to have "praised YHWH God
of Israel (*běqōl qādōl lěmā 'ălāh*) with a great raised voice." The
final word in the Hebrew, *lěmā 'ălāh* rendered "raised," is, in
fact, different from *ma 'ălāh* the singular of *ma 'ălōt*, "ascents,"
and is not convincing as an explanation of the superscription.
Luther may have accepted this theory, if we understand his
translation, *"ein Lied im hohern Chor,"* "a song for the higher
choir" in the sense of "in louder (= higher) tones." Others un-
derstand Luther's translation of the psalm title as "a song for a
choir in a high place (= a raised platform)."

6. H. T. Armfield, drawing upon *Midrash Tehillim*, inter-
prets "ascents" not as the emergence from Babylonian captivity
"but the goings up out of any trouble or distress," hence, the
plural "goings up" not the "going up."[7] Armfield further sup-
ports his argument by appealing to the first term in the super-
scription, *šīr*, "song." The verbal form of that word appears in
Jer 20:13, "Sing unto YHWH, praise YHWH, for he has saved (=
delivered) the soul of the poor from the hand of evildoers." It is
appropriate, therefore, according to this theory, that the super-
scription be rendered "Songs of Deliverances" since songs are
used in the context of deliverances and the plural accords with
the several deliverances experienced by the Israelites.

7. One further understanding of the superscription has been
espoused particularly by the early and medieval Christian com-
mentators. In this approach the "ascents" are taken as the rise
to "the higher walks of faith"; "advance in the spiritual life. . .to
the presence of God."[8] The content of Pss 120-134 are inter-
preted as evidencing this religious progress. There is no literal
evidence of *ma 'ălōt* meaning spiritual progress. There is, how-
ever, the suggestion that "raising" the hands and eyes, from the
stem *ns'* (Ps 121:1 and 123:1) and "from the depths" (Ps 130:1)
imply "ascent" and therefore the heading is deemed
appropriate.

The variety of explanations of *šīr hamma 'ălōt* underscores

---

[5] J. Baker and E. W. Nicholson, *The Commentary of Rabbi David Kimḥe on Psalms cxx-cl* (Cambridge: At the University Press, 1973) 3.

[6] RaDaQ commentary on Ps 120:1 in Rabbinic Bible (*Miqra' ot Gedolot*).

[7] H. T. Armfield, *The Gradual Psalms: A Treatise on the Fifteen Songs of Degrees with Commentary* (London: J. T. Hayes, 1874) 14.

[8] J. M. Neale and R. F. Littledale, *A Commentary on the Psalms from Primitive and Medieval Writers*, vol. IV (London: Joseph Masters & Co., 1883) 166.

the vagueness and uncertainty of the term and also elucidates some common features of the psalms bearing this designation. The most widely accepted understanding of these psalms is as songs sung by pilgrims going up to Jerusalem on the three annual festivals. We may construe them thus on the basis of the explicit evidence in some of the psalms and by interpretation of intimations in others. Pss 122:1-4; 125:1-5; 129:5 and 134:1-3 particularly relate to Zion as the site at the end of a pilgrimage. Some psalms still seem to remain unrelated to pilgrimages. William R. Taylor and W. Stewart McCullough account for these by proposing that "the collection has in the course of time broadened into something like a handbook of devotions for the use of pilgrims."[9]

## BOUNDARY MARKERS

The immediate environment of the collection further underscores its integrity and autonomy. Within a work of art, the parts are essentially incomplete; they seek completion in their relatedness to the other parts and to the whole. Similarly, the text as a whole looks for its completion to similar texts with which it may form a series or to a compositional type of which it may be a variant. Pss 120-134 exhibit relationships among their hierarchically organized parts and between themselves and the larger body of psalm texts in which they are embedded. In Gerald H. Wilson's examination of editorial efforts to combine and unify originally unrelated groups of psalms, he looked closely at the seams between the collections where editorial activity is most evident.[10] By following the same approach of studying the seams, we recognize structural indications of the integrity and autonomy of the Songs of Ascents.

Ps 134, the final Song of Ascent, formally signals the conclusion of this Psalter within the Psalter. The closural element is its doxological wording, *bārĕkū 'et YHWH*, "Bless YHWH," in vv 1 and 2 and *yĕbārekĕkā YHWH miṣṣiyyōn*, "YHWH will bless you out of Zion," in v 3. Noteworthy also is the fivefold repetition of YHWH in the span of the mere three verses and twenty-five words of the psalm.

At the conclusion of each of the first four of the five divisions into which Psalms is divided, a doxology appears that structurally concludes the section. Ps 41:14, 72:19, 89:53 and 106:48

---

[9] *IB* 4 (New York: Abingdon Press, 1955) 639.
[10] G. H. Wilson, *The Editing of the Hebrew Psalter* (Chico, Calif.: Scholars Press, 1985) 5.

present these closing doxologies. A review of the formal variations among these verses allows us to admit Ps 134 as a variant within the range of this same closural doxology convention. As such, its placement at the end of the Songs of Ascents brings the small collection to a close. I understand Wilson's comment about this closural device to encompass Ps 134 also: ". . .the occurrence of the doxologies is certainly *not* fortuitous, but represent[s] editorially induced method[s] of giving "shape" to the pss corpus."[11]

Wilson cites analogues from Mesopotamian hymns and catalogues in which "praise" and "blessing" conclude documents and sections within documents. For Hebrew hymnic literature to exhibit a similar technique is therefore not surprising.

Ps 134 is, after Ps 117, the shortest in the Psalter. Ps 134 contains only an invitation to praise YHWH and a blessing given by Him. It is less a psalm than a single liturgical formula. Felix Bovet expressed it this way, "Il [Ps 134] ne serait là que pour marquer la fin des chants de pèlerinage et leur servir de doxologie."[12]

There is a tension between the setting apart of Ps 134 from what follows and some verbal correspondences that link Ps 134 with Ps 135 (cf. 134:1 and 135:1-2; 134:3 and 135:21). Opposing pulls result—one toward separation and one toward linkage. This tension is an example of artistry in the design of the entire book of Psalms. If Pss 120-134 and other groups were entirely self-contained within the Psalter, the larger work would be fragmented into several incompatible subunits. The designer of the artistic whole of Psalms provided some demarcations of smaller units and some threads of continuity across the demarcations.

The opening of the Songs of Ascents is also structurally set apart from what precedes it. Ps 119 is the longest psalm among the MT 150. This one psalm of 176 verses contrasts strikingly to the brief *šîr hamma'ălôt* psalms, comprising a total of 101 verses among it 15 psalms. Ps 119 is also an acrostic poem which further distinguishes it from the Songs of Ascents and from most biblical poetry. This poetic structural oddity serves as a closural device immediately preceding our small collection. The final chapter of Proverbs, too, exhibits a variation of form in its acrostic design. Closural devices and boundary markers set the Songs of Ascents apart from their neighboring psalms. The longest psalm in the Psalter in an acrostic form ends what precedes the

---

[11] Ibid., 186.
[12] F. Bovet, *Les Psaumes de Maaloth* (Paris: Neuchatel, 1889) 202.

collection; Ps 134, the second to the shortest psalm in the Psalter concludes the Songs of Ascents with a recognized closural doxology.

My identification of various devices that set off Pss 120-134 from the psalms directly adjacent to them does not preclude there being other configurations of the total book of Psalms that bind the Songs of Ascents into other groupings. It is precisely this type of shifting perceptions of textual configuration that creates the tension in the work of art. Viewed from one perspective, part A is dominant; from another vantage part B rises in prominence; from a third position, the whole is paramount.

## INDIVIDUAL SONGS OF ASCENTS

The common title, the consecutive placement of the fifteen psalms, their formal difference from the preceding Ps 119 and the closural doxology in Ps 134, all establish the autonomy of the collection as a whole. We turn now to the individual members of the collection. In this section, I present explications of some of the more prominent centripetal forces at work within the discrete Songs of Ascents. Since these forces do not operate in isolation, I examine several of the psalms, concentrating on the interaction of the elements within each. The reader perceives a tightness of structure in the individual Songs of Ascents as a result of the interlocking of the elements. Among the compositional features responsible for this apperception are the general brevity of the pieces, the characteristic narrow compass of the semantic field, and the repetition devices in their various forms. The numerous repetition formulae include: the reiteration of a word or phrase several times in consecutive verses, the restatement of synonyms or near synonyms, the rehearsal of identical syntactic forms, and the repeated collocation of a significant keyword or leitmotif. A further repetitive device is the inclusio. This figure features a significant word or phrase at the open and close of the work or section. The inclusio sets boundaries and provides a satisfying sense of closure and completeness to the unit.

I do not presume to present an exhaustive identification of the unifying features. I do aim at making clear the nature of the phenomenon of centripetal and centrifugal elements at work in the Songs of Ascents.

*Psalm 120*

Ps 120 is an excellent example of a major structuring princi-

ple of the various Songs of Ascents. It is therefore well placed as
the first in this collection. It is also appropriate to examine it
first. The brief poem expresses a basic idea and elaborates upon
it in terms of closely related imagery and repetition of words
that suggest interlocking meanings.

The psalmist of Ps 120 expresses the distress of the Israelite
living among an alien people. The perfidious tongue of the god-
less is one of the dominant themes of the poem. Deadly arrows,
the artist's metaphor for the malicious speech is a second theme
of the poem. The obvious relatedness of the two themes makes
for a dense unifying structure. Speech as arrows, and speech
and arrows, are the two dominant motifs of the poem. Both the
tenor and the vehicle are developed into themes.

> Unto YHWH, in my straits, I called and He answered me
> (120:1)

The entreaty to YHWH and His response are both framed in
verbal terms. Although the spoken plea is an oft-employed ap-
peal, the psalmists do record other means and postures in calling
upon God (cf. 121:6 and 123:1, raising of eyes; 77:3, gesturing
with hands and [eyes] flowing; 77:4, moaning; and 77:6, recol-
lecting the past, etc.). The artist in 120, however, uses speech
terminology and builds with it a unity of figure. The next verse
makes this concentration apparent.

> Lord, save my soul from the lying *lips* and the deceiving
> *tongue.* (120:2)

The psalmist's distress is the falsehood and treachery emanating
from the organs of speech. V. 3 is not fully clear and has been
understood variously:

> What can you profit, what can you gain, O deceitful
> tongue? (*NJPS*)

> How he will give you! How he will add to you! O treach-
> erous tongue. (AB)

> What has he in store for you, slanderous tongue? What
> more has he for you? (*NEB*)

> What shall be given to you? And what more shall be done
> to you, deceitful tongue? (*RSV*)

The differences not withstanding, there is no discrepancy in the understanding of *lāšōn rĕmiyyāh*—"deceitful, treacherous, slanderous *tongue*." We note in v 3 not only the direct repetition of the term *lāšōn rĕmiyyāh* from v 2, which is a characteristic stylistic device of the Songs of Ascents, but also that the particular phrase is one that insists on the reader's attention to the figures of "speech." The reiteration and the specific term reiterated both exert a unifying and centralizing force on the psalm. The artist persists in the elaboration of the speech figure in v 4 by introducing a metaphor for the malicious tongue which develops the theme further. The poet likens the slanderous tongue to a warrior's sharpened arrows tipped with burning coals. The analogy is a felicitous one despite its conventionality. The sinner and a burning fire on the lips is pictured in Prov 16:27. The tongue of the evildoer is also compared to a sharpened sword and the word to an "arrow" in Ps 64:4. Jer 9:7 likens the sinner's tongue to an "arrow" and Jer 9:2 depicts the tongue as a "bow." The use of traditional equations such as evil tongue, lips and speech to sword, arrow and bow is typical of Psalms. This psalm draws from the same literary store.

There are few innovative, daring and extravagant metaphors in the Psalter. The greatness of Psalms emerges despite its choice of established analogies. The familiar locution, the fixed analogy and conservative compositional pattern are more in evidence in Psalms than in the other poetical books in Scripture. The originality and genius of the psalmists/poets lie in part in their slight shift of the convention. They rely on the well-worn but invest it with a subtle newness. This nuance in the traditional averts a fall into banality while adhering to the customary mold. The retardation of the flow of the work without a break in the sequentiality of the poem is a peculiar artistic achievement of the psalmists.

Ps 120:4 bears this out. V 4 applies the well attested image of arrows to the malicious tongue. The artistry shines forth first in the Hebrew adjective selected, *šĕnūnīm*, "sharpened." The English, "sharpened" does not carry the effect of the Hebrew. The Hebrew word *šĕnūnīm* derives from *šnn*, "tooth." The poet thus suggests a complete set: lip (v 2) tongue (vv 2, 3), and now tooth (v 4).[13] The artist thereby underscores this theme of treacherous speech.

The reader is further impressed by a wordplay in v 3 that becomes apparent only after reading v 4. The term *lāšōn*

---

[13] M. Dahood, *Psalms III*, AB 17a (Garden City, N.Y.: Doubleday, 1970) 197.

*rĕmiyyāh* translated as "deceitful tongue" carries within it the intimation of "arrow" also. The root *rmh* in the *pi'ēl* signifies "cheat," "beguile." In the basic *qal*, however, *rmh* denotes "cast" or "shoot." Ex 15:1 and 21 have *rāmāh bayyām*, "he cast into the sea," and more appropriate yet, Jer 4:29 has *rōmēh qešet*, "bow-shooter," "bowman," and Ps 78:9 *rōmēy qešet*, "bow-shooters," "bowmen." With this wordplay the poet suggests a linkage of the tenor or referent, "deceitful tongue," with the vehicle or metaphor, "arrows." Upon conclusion of v 4, in which explicit mention of arrows is made, the correspondence is also highlighted. The reader reprocesses the information given in vv 2 and 3 and sees the twofold etymology of *rmh*. The retroactive supplying of additional significance is in conformity with Robert Alter's notion that

> . . .poetry, working through a system of complex linkages of sound, image, word, rhythm, syntax, theme, idea, is an instrument for conveying densely patterned meanings, sometimes contradictory meanings, that are not readily conveyable through other kinds of discourse.[14]

The creator of Ps 120 succeeds in artistic play with subtle literary linkages.

Vv 5-7 open with the impassioned exclamation of grief *'ōyāh*, "Woe!" It is noteworthy that this *hapax legomenon* exhibits the accusative ending *āh* as does *ṣārātāh*, "straits," at the open of the psalm in v 1. It thus functions as a type of grammatical refrain or echo that recalls the beginning of the work.

> Woe is me that I sojourn in Meschech,
> [That] I dwell in the tents of Kedar. (120:5)

Scholarly opinion holds that Meshech and Kedar are two regions far removed from Jerusalem and also from one another. Meshech, as mentioned in Gen 10:2, Ezek 27:13 and 32:26, points to a location between the Black Sea and the Caspian Sea; "Kedar," appearing in Gen 25:13 and Isa 42:11, indicates a tribe of nomads in the Arabian Desert. The artist employs "Meshech" and "Kedar" in 120:5 not as specific geographical designations but emblematically. The pair, Meshech and Kedar, is to be taken as a merism expressing the totality of the menacing diaspora, even its most far-flung regions.

The artist exhibits another clever interlocking device by

---

[14] Alter, *Poetry*, 113.

specifying "Meshech" and "Kedar" and not another pair of equally distant sites. Meshech carries a significant resonance. In 1 Kgs 22:34 (= 2 Chron 18:33) and Isa 66:19, *mšk* appears with "bow" as its complement and denotes "draw the bow" or "bowmen." Isa 21:17 presents "the mighty men of the children of Kedar" also as archers. Ps 120:5 thus picks up the image of the bow and arrow mentioned in v 4 and evoked in v 3 and v 2. The subtle paronomasia and ethnic allusions are centripetal features binding the various levels of the work.

The compactness and density of the poem result from the repeated recalling of words and images mentioned earlier in the poem. Explicit reiteration and artful suggestions of already stated elements combine to produce a unified and focused composition so characteristic of the Songs of Ascents.

V 6 begins with an unusual form, *rabbat*, "much," "great" or "long." The unconventional *rabbat* for the more common *rabbāh* resembles the construct although it does not carry that sense. Cyrus H. Gordon has shown in Proverbs that "it was a favorite stunt in presenting ancient riddles to alert the reader through an incorrect form."[15] Although we are not dealing with riddles in Ps 120, perhaps an intentional use of double-entendre is signalled by this strange form. The persistent evocation of archery and bowmen throughout the poem may continue into v 6. In Prov 26:10, *rb* denotes "archer." In Jer 50:29, *rabbīm* means "archers" and is used in parallelism with *dōrkē gešet*, "drawers of the bow." In Job 16:13 *rabbāyw* signifies "his" or "its archers." The multiple wordplay is intricate and all centers on the themes of the poem.

*rabbat*, for more common *rabbāh*, also summons to mind the opening word of distress *ṣārātāh* (v 1) for *ṣārāh*. This is another example of a grammatical cue to recall an earlier word and to ensure greater unity in the work.

The closing verse of the psalm reinforces contrasts between the psalmist and the godless, and between peace and war. Both contrasts the poet expresses in terms of the speech and arrow motifs of the poem.

> I am [for] peace but, when I speak, they are for war.
> (120:7)

The speech of the psalmist is the antithesis of the speech of the godless. This final line of the poem is to be read in the light of

---

[15] C. H. Gordon, "New Light on the Hebrew Language," *Hebrew Abstracts* 15 (1974) 29.

what preceded it. The closing word "war" evokes all the means of war mentioned and suggested throughout the psalm. His speech is [for] peace; their speech is sharpened arrows shot from bows drawn by mighty archers. This suggestive recapitulation in the final line, of the motifs of the poem, is a device that knits the threads into a tight weave.

A uniform tone of despair brings the work to a stylistic and thematic integration. Theme and structure combine to convey the unity. Six of the seven verses in the psalm end with terms of adversity. Only the first verse shows any positive glimmer; the final six verses treat the powers of evil besetting the psalmist. The concluding words of these verses reverberate:

> . . .deceitful tongue (v 2)
> . . .deceitful tongue (v 3)
> . . .burning coals of the broom tree (v 4)
> . . .the tents of Kedar (v 5)
> . . .enemy of peace (v 6)
> . . .they are for war (v 7)

The terms rise to a crescendo from the mere (!) "deceitful tongue" to "war." Indeed, the Hebrew *hēmmāh lammilḥāmāh*, "they are for war," are the echoing sounds heard even after the poem is completed. Attention to the difference in tone expressed in v 1 and vv 2-7 leads us to understand that v 1 is a recollection of a former calamity, a call and a deliverance that the psalmist experienced at an earlier time. V 2 begins a new call for assistance in the current distress besetting him. The earlier deliverance leads the psalmist to renew his cry for help.

Despite the marked closeness in which the motifs and their elaborations are gathered together, the psalmist eschews a complete closedness that would form a self-contained unit allowing no expansion. Various elements of the present psalm lead to others in the Songs of Ascents collection. The unconventional locutions: *baṣṣārātāah*, "in straits," *'ōyāh*, "woe!" and *rabbat*, "long" or "much," point to each other but also invoke numerous analogous dialectical elements in Pss 120-134. For example, *rabbat* recurs in 134:4, 129:1 and again in 129:2. The picture of the warrior and his sharpened arrows finds a similar image in 127:4. The poet employs the stylistic device of stairlike parallelism here and in Pss 121, 122 and 123. This is a feature whereby the artist repeats in successive verses, a word or phrase from the preceding verse. The interlocking, ascending result accounts for the designations "stairlike," "staircase" or "incremental" pattern. In Ps 120, *lāšōn rĕmiyyāh* (v 2) is recalled in v 3; *šākantī*‾in v 5 is taken up in *šākĕnāh* of v 6; *šālōm* of v 6 is reiterated in v 7. This recurring repetition pattern in Pss 120-134 induced some to assign a technical meaning to the term "Songs of Ascents" in which "ascents" refers to the "steps" up the "staircase." The particular effect within each individual poem demonstrating this parallelism formula is compacting and recapitulating. The reader does not go afield but constantly returns to the point of departure, and is thus kept at tight rein. The recurrence of this distinctive device in several proximate psalms also ties the works to one another, creating a larger unity. The brevity of Ps 120 also finds its analogy in the other Songs of Ascents.

To tally is impossible—but to recognize is important. The composition of the psalm is tight but the links with other Psalms of Ascents exert their force as well.

## Psalm 121

Ps 121 is characteristic of the other Songs of Ascents in several respects. Brevity is one. Although not the shortest, it covers only eight verses. Many of the psalms are of similar length (cf. Pss 1, 3, 4, 11, 13, 14, 15, 23, etc.).

The heading on Ps 121 differs slightly from the heading of the others in the collection—"Song *for* the Ascents" and not "Song *of* the Ascents." The particular nuance of this variation— if indeed there is any—is unknown today and does not seem significant. The superscription, variation notwithstanding, is a second characteristic of the Songs of Ascents and links Ps 121 to them.

The thematic scope of this psalm and the others in the small collection is limited. One theme or image is presented and repeated, almost played with. Various aspects of the one motif are revealed. The work, nevertheless, remains focused and modest in thematic range. The brevity, common heading, and thematic concentration, are three centripetal factors in each examplar of the entire collection seeming to tie all together.

As we turn our attention to Ps 121 alone, the great economy of means is immediately apparent. The poet does not introduce the time and place. The setting has been described by some commentators (such as Keet) as the approach of pilgrims to Jerusalem. They espy the Judean hills and long for the sight of Zion. Others, such as Kittel, have drawn on the tradition of facing Jerusalem during prayer (cf. 1 Kgs 8:44 and 48, and Dan 6:9-12) and have considered the psalmist far from Jerusalem but directing prayer to that Holy Place from afar. The two contradictory interpretations both rest on the centrality of Zion in the psalm and to the ancient Israelite. The vagueness of the text also allows for the two views. All that is established is the mountainous terrain (v 1). Neither the speaker, nor the one who seems to respond in the second person (in v 3) is identified. This two-person understanding is not universally accepted but the pattern of pairing certain verses may indicate an antiphonal psalm form or a possible dialogue. A hesitant questioner may utter v 1, while a staunchly faithful listener responds in v 2. Vv 3 and 4 similarly constitute a pair with a repetition of the two final words of v 3 in v 4. The vagueness notwithstanding, the compactness of the psalm is manifest.

The centripetal force of the poem finds its expression also in complementary repetitions. The stem *šmr*, "protect," "guard," appears six times in vv 3-8. The second person pronomial suffix, *-kā*, "you" or "your," occurs ten times in vv 3-8. Their combined occurrence is also remarkable. No fewer than six times the suffix *-kā*, "you" or "your," is affixed to the stem *šmr* or to a direct object that *šmr* governs. Furthermore, the explicit use of YHWH is seen four times. Indeed, these noteworthy multiple recurrences and the close association of "you" or "your," "guard" or "protect" and "YHWH" underscore the theme of personal protection and security that YHWH provides. Any sense of dispassionate abstract, theoretical pronouncements is averted in this psalm by the tenfold reiteration of the personal pronoun. There is also a tenfold use of verbs whose subject is YHWH or an epithet for YHWH. The abundance of such repetitions knits the text into a dense structural and thematic fabric.

There is a further structural device that unites the distinct parts. As in Ps 120, a particular word or words is used in one verse and then reiterated in the next verse. Thus 121:1 ends with the word 'ezrī, "my help," and v 2 begins with this same word. V 3 ends with the three words 'al yānūm šŏmĕrekā, "He will not slumber, your guardian." V 4 picks up these words and employs them: hinnēh lo' yānūm . . . šōmēr yiśrāēl, "behold He does not slumber. . . the guardian of Israel." Vv 7 and 8 are similarly linked by the staircase pattern: YHWH yismŏrĕkā, "YHWH will protect you," and YHWH yišmōr ṣē'tĕkā, "YHWH will protect your going forth."

The narrowly circumscribed range of imagery in this psalm is also a unifying force. Consider by way of contrast the far-ranging rapidly changing metaphors in Song of Songs. In that work the disjointedness is conspicuous. In Ps 121 the controlling theme is the outdoor trek with its inherent dangers and the trust in the protectiveness of YHWH. Each verse treats this single motif: assistance is sought as the traveler beholds the mountains (v 1). YHWH, the maker of the heavens and earth is affirmed as the source of that assistance (v 2). The ever vigilant protector will not permit the traveler's foot to stumble (v 3). The protector's untiring solicitude (v 4) will provide shade and will constantly be with him (v 5). By day and night He will prevent the elements from harming the traveler (v 6). He will protect body and soul from all dangers (v 7), upon leaving and returning, now and forever (v 8). All the imagery is borrowed from the same semantic field.

The concentration on a journey and the inclusion of this psalm in the Songs of Ascents has strengthened the interpretation of the trip as a pilgrimage and the mountains of v 1 as those around Jerusalem. No mention, however, is made of pilgrims or of the Holy City.

V 1 and v 8 contain a verbal and thematic inclusion which further tightens the composition. V 1 *mē'ayin yābō'*, "whence comes," is seconded in v 8 *ṣē'těkā ūbō'ekā*, "your going and your coming." On the semantic level, the psalmist conceives of YHWH's providence both in the temporal and the spatial dimensions. The Lord is "the maker of the heaven and the earth" (v 2); He will act "from now and forever" (v 8). The two antithetical pairs, one in the realm of space (v 2) and the other in the domain of time (v 8) echo one another, providing a complement to the journey theme and the reliance on divine protection throughout.

Other forms of antithesis mark this psalm and bind it together. The conventional polar pairs are formulaic and trite. The mention of one element evokes the other. The reader does not need to wonder at the connection. Heaven and earth (v 2), day and night (v 6), sun and moon (v 6), coming and going (v 8), and now and forever (v 8) are all stereotyped polar pairs. "Now and forever" recurs in the Songs of Ascents alone three times (121:8; 125:2; 131:3) as does "Maker of heaven and earth" (121:2; 124:8; 134:3). The conventionality indicates a constancy that is an attribute of the Lord's protectiveness. The polarities also highlight the infinite range of YHWH's protective activity. The structure thus reflects, complements, and reinforces the content.

Vv 1-3 not only display repetition of words that lead to the subsequent line and back but also exhibit alternating directional cues that direct the reader's gaze.

v 1   I *raise* my eyes to the *mountains*      [up]
v 2       maker of *heaven*                     [up]
          and *earth*                           [down]
v 3   . . .your *foot* to stumble               [down]

V 1 is clearly oriented upwards. V 2 includes the formulaic locution "heaven and earth" which first guides the eyes upward and then immediately diverts attention downward. The invoking of the stumbling foot again is a downward orientation.

Another knitting device in vv 1 and 2 is the ambiguity in the sense of the word *mē 'ayin*, "whence."

### Whence comes my help (v 1)

Ps 121:1 read alone calls for a declarative sense of the word "whence" explaining the reason for the psalmist's raising of eyes to the mountains, i.e., it is from the mountains that help will come. The reader then advances to v 2 and modifies the understanding of the word. V 2 supplies an answer to what now appears to have been a question, "Whence comes my help?" The particle *mē 'ayin* is generally taken in a strictly interrogative sense as in Gen 29:4: "And Jacob said to them, 'My brother, from where (*mē 'ayin*) are you?' " Josh 2:4 may be adduced as a justification of the use of the particle as a relative: "And the woman took the two men and hid them and said thus, 'There came men to me, but I knew not from where (*mē 'ayin*) they were.' " Even here the word in question might be functioning as an indirect interrogative. The slight vagueness, however, allows for equivocation.

### My help comes from the Lord. . . (v 2)

The setting of the eyes on the mountains will be of no avail; none can help except YHWH. Is this an answer to a question in v 1? Or is it an affirmation in the face of a misguided statement in v 1?

When considered in light of what precedes it, "whence" has a declarative sense; when regarded in terms of what follows it, "whence" has an interrogative sense. Such "double-duty" usage has much in common with what Gordon has called "Janus-faced parallelism" and has described as a device that "hinges on the use of a single word with two entirely different meanings: one meaning paralleling what precedes, and the other meaning what follows.''[16] It enriches the poetry and leads to a mental doubling back and centripetality of the segment.

The artist employs another unifying device that keeps the reader closely connected with the work. From time to time the psalmist inverts the usual syntax. The reader now remains with the text expectantly until the full meaning becomes clear. This use of *casus pendens* exerts a centripetal force. Vv 3 and 4, for example, withhold disclosure of the subject until the end of the verse. This grammatical device focuses the attention of the reader on the work and on the progress of the sentence. Small self-contained units lead to a staccato, less cohesive reading. The joining of sentences, ideas, and phrases smoothes and connects the text.

## Psalm 122

Repetitions of sounds and words can be a strongly unifying feature. In Ps 122, the restatements are not merely arbitrary reduplications. The reiterations are used artistically; they turn the composition inward and reinforce the theme.

The preeminent theme of the psalm is *yĕrūšālēm*, "Jerusalem." The major centripetal devices in this psalm are varieties of repetition that focus on Jerusalem. Assonance and paronomasia or the suggestive repetition of similar sounds function as such prominent devices. The psalmist plays on the name Jerusalem in several phonologically related words. Whatever the true etymology of "Jerusalem" may be, the wordplays and sound-plays in this psalm express the popular folk etymology which associates *yĕrūšālēm* with "city of *šālōm*," "city of peace." Vv 6 and 7 carry the punning to an extreme:

> *ša 'ǎlū šĕlōm yĕrūšālēm*
> *yišlāyū 'ōhǎbāyik* (v 6)
> *yĕhī šālōm bĕḥēylēk*
> *šalwāh bĕ'armĕnōtāyik* (v 7)
> Pray for the peace of Jerusalem!
> May they be tranquil, your lovers. (v 6)
> May there be peace within your ramparts
> Tranquility in your citadels. (v 7)

The poet appears to enjoy employing the assonant words that interweave the themes and sounds of praying, peace, tranquility and Jerusalem. *yĕrūšālēm*, "Jerusalem," *šālōm*, "peace,"

---

[16] C. H. Gordon, "New Directions," *BASP* 15 (1978) 59. Cf. G. A. Rendsburg, "Janus Parallelism in Gen 49:26: *JBL* 99 (1980) 291-93.

šalwāh, "tranquility," and yišlāyū, "may they be tranquil," share the š, the l, and the long vowel sound.

The concept of peace and tranquility emerges as chief motif complementing the theme of Jerusalem. On the compositional level each of the sound-related words calls to mind (or to ear) the other members of the phonetic family. Lamentations 1-4 employ the acrostic structure which joins the lines in a recognizable pattern that produces a set—the alphabet. The poet of Ps 122 also creates a recognizable set—a set of š, l and m sounds. These sounds recall the Jerusalem, tranquility and peace themes. The artist further invokes these sounds in vv 4 and 5: šešām . . . lěšēm. . .šămmāh.[17]

The limits of the work are clearly defined by the inclusio bēyt YHWH, "the house of YHWH," in vv 1 and 9. The inclusio also introduces the second motif, related to the first motif and to the main theme. A pilgrimage to the "House of YHWH" in "Jerusalem," the "City of Peace," emerges as the controlling motif of the poem. The dense interlaced weave is obvious. The mention of bēyt, YHWH, šālōm, or yěrūšālēm in the poem cannot be understood but in light of the other three. The poet foregrounds the prominence of the terms by repeating each one three times. No other term in this psalm merits the significant threefold restatement.

Luis Alonso-Schökel noted another expressive repetition device in this psalm.[18] Five cola in the final four verses end with a feminine singular pronominal suffix: 'ōhăbāyik, "your lovers," ḥēylēk, "your rampart," 'armĕnōtāyik, "your citadels," bāk, "in you," and lāk, "for you." This concentration of second person feminine singular pronouns indicating direct address to Jerusalem conveys a strong personal relationship between the psalmist and the city. The themes of the work are strengthened by the introduction of a grammatical indicator of the poet's affinity to the city. Moreover, the insistent fivefold recurrence of the form links the cola in their function as direct address to the City of Peace.

*Psalm 123*

The brevity, simplicity and limited range of Ps 123 gives it,

---

[17] On sound and meaning, cf. A. Berlin, "Motif and Creativity in Biblical Poetry" (*Prooftexts* 3 [1983] 237-38).

[18] L. Alonso-Schökel, *Treinta salmos: poesía y oración*, Estudios de Antiguo Testamento 2 (Madrid: Ediciones Cristianidad, 1981) 301.

too, a tight centripetal orientation. The opening words of the psalm,

> To you I raise my eyes, O enthroned one in heaven
> (123:1)

recall the beginning of Ps 121,

> I raise my eyes to the mountains whence comes my help
> (121:1).

The poet of Ps 123 organizes the composition around a series of polarities. The pull of each pole is balanced by its counterpart. The theme of the psalm arises from the relationships of the various antitheses.

The psalmist presents the basic proposition in v 1, a dichotomy with a definite directional cue. The poet, here on earth below, raises eyes heavenward to the enthroned one on high. The psalmist then elaborates on this relationship of the heavenly god and the earthly human. Two similes framed in terms of contrarieties expand the relationship. The focus of the psalm is the mystery of the bridge connecting the two poles. V 2 ends with an explanation of the similes in a restatement of the basic proposition. The unity of the poem is reinforced again, as in Ps 121, by the repetitions. We note the compactness of the psalm in a fourfold formulation of the one fundamental assertion. The first likens the look of the faithful toward God in heaven to the servants' regard of the hand of their lords. A primary point of comparison is certainly subservience and dominance. Having introduced a directional cue in the basic proposition by the words,

> To You I *raise* my eyes O enthroned one in *heaven*; (v 1),

the poet persists to evoke a sense of spatiality in the figurative reformulations:

> Behold, as the eyes of the servants are toward the hand
>   of their lords,
> As the eyes of a maid are toward the hand of her
>   mistress, (v 2)

These two similes suggest the literal and figurative sense of a *lowly* slave looking *up* at the hand of the *overlord* and the *underling lifting* her gaze to her *ascendant* lady. The continuation of v 2 includes the fourth formulation of the theme which makes the comparison explicit. Thus four parallel iterations comprise one half of the psalm.

The poet fashions these two verses in particularly interlocking ways. A chiastic ordering of the lines ties them tightly together:

| v 1 | To You I raise my eyes, O enthroned one in heaven | -proposition A |
| v 2 | Behold, as the eyes of servants are toward the hand of their lords | -comparison B |
| | As the eyes of the maid are toward the hand or her mistress | -comparison B' |
| | Thus our eyes are toward YHWH our God | -proposition A' |

Another chiastic arrangement rests on the ordering of the objects of the gazes: the first and fourth are the deity, the second and third are human.

The structure of these four lines of vv 1-2 is yet more intricate and interlaced. Repetition with variation is a favored biblical technique. Verbatim restatement rarely advances the argument; a subtle change in a repeated phrase calls attention to itself and to the implicit differences. In each case the artist varied the grammatical person and number. Deliberate gender and number matching results. In each line the number and gender of the subject and object conform. Chiasm is also apparent. Lines 1 and 4 are first person; 2 and 3 are third person.

A     My (m.s.) eyes toward You (m.s.)
B.    eyes of servants (m.p.) toward their lords (m.p.)
B'    eyes of maid (f.s.) toward her lady (f.s.)
A'    our (m.p.) eyes toward YHWH our God (m.p. in form)

On another level, the shifts from first person singular to second person masculine singular, to third person masculine plural to third person feminine singular to first person plural introduce something that a more consistent series would lack. The statement becomes a broader truth—a hint of the universal. The proposition applies, not just to "him" or to "them" but to "me" and "us" and "her," too.

The second half of the psalm (vv 3-4) elucidates the meaning of the gaze. The transition to v 3 is not merely thematic and logical. An impressive threefold repetition of the verbal stem

*ḥnn* "to be gracious" forms the segue. The final two words of v
2 provide the reason for the look—"until He-be-gracious-unto-
us." The reader now can complete the analysis of the preceding
cola. Until now, the motivation has been withheld. The wonder
as to the meaning of the fixing of the gaze has mounted. The
first three words at the head of v 3 include the same verb twice
in the imperative, "Be-gracious-unto-us!" separated by the
vocative YHWH. The artistry is noteworthy: "He-will-be-
gracious-unto-us" and "Be-gracious-unto-us" have the identical
consonantal and vocalic spelling save for a preformative *yōd* on
the former.

Is the explanation of the fixing of the gaze on the master's
hand the fear of punishment at his hand or the anticipation of a
cessation of punishment? Is it the provision of food or a silent
order or wish made known through a movement of the hand or
is it protection provided by the master? Complete
understanding of vv 1 and 2, delayed until the end of the fourth
parallel statement, now emerges. The motivation for the
insistent stare is now grasped. The reader subliminally supplies
the words "until he be gracious unto me/us/her/them" to the
preceding lines. The loose ends are picked up and tucked back
into the tight weave.

Vv 3 and 4 continue the use of repetition:

> . . . *kī rab śāba 'nū būz*
> *rabbat śābĕ'āh lāh napšēnū* . . .
> . . . for we are fully sated (with) contempt (v 3)
> fully sated is our soul. . . . (v 4)

The biblical preference for modified restatement is again
apparent. The essence of the pronouncement is the same
although the word *rab* in v 3, translated as "fully," becomes
*rabat* in v 4. This latter form is rare but constitutes no
substantial semantic difference (cf. 120:6; 129:1, 2). The shift in
the subject of the verb "to be sated" from "we" in v 3, to "our
soul" in v 4 is also to be noted. The psalm comes to a close with
an expansion of the object of the satiety. V 3 relates that "we
are fully sated with contempt"; v 4 develops this idea with the
furtherance of the sentiment of contempt: "the mockery of the
complacent" and "the contempt of the proud."

The psalm closes with the mention of the "complacent" and
the "proud"—the earthly antithesis of the opening word "to
You," the deity enthroned in heaven. The initial appeal to
YHWH on high is made because of the contempt and mockery

of the complacent and proud down below. Perhaps the poet deliberately chose the strange word *lig'ēyōnīm* for "the proud" because of its derivation from the stem *g'h* meaning "high".

An additional unifying device akin to repetition is operative here. The poet uses numerous analogous grammatical forms throughout this short psalm. These related forms recall one another. Note, in particular, the abundant employment of the pronominal suffix—ten times in the four verses.

On the phonological level the structure is also dense. The relatively close juxtaposition of similar sounds at the end of the composition tightens the whole and functions somewhat like rhyme. V 4b and 4c end in *-im*; 3a and 4a end in *-nū*; and *-ēynū* occurs three times in line 2c alone.

### Psalm 124

Psalm 124 exhibits vivid and varying metaphors. The use of this type of analogy is in contrast to the concentrated related metaphors typical of the Songs of Ascents. The strong congruence of analogy in Ps 124 keeps the psalm centralized. On the thematic level, congruence of metaphor provides a centripetality. The artist of Ps 124, nevertheless, prevents the composition from falling into disjointedness. The images however diverse they may be, are related and brought within a unified compass. The treatment of the metaphors along with the careful employment of unifying structural components produces another Psalm of Ascent with a concentrated focus.

The first five verses of this eight-verse composition are held together by a series of logical propositions. Each one is clearly marked as such by its opening word(s): "had it not been. . ." and "then. . ." or "therefore. . . ." These external signals cement the work. As soon as the first "had it not been. . ." is recorded, its resolution is sought in what ensues. The second verse, however, does not bring the proposition to a close. V 2 maintains and even raises the suspense by withholding that resolution. In its place, v 2 rehearses the protasis of v 1, amplifying it with the adverbial phrase "when man rose up against us." The reader is anxious to learn what, indeed, would have happened "had it not been YHWH who was with/for us when man rose up against Israel" (v 2). The apodosis of the twice-uttered conditional clause first appears in v 3. A tentative closure is reached—tentative only because v 4 repeats the term *'ăzay*, "then," which introduces a second consequence. The artist-logician thus extends the tightly structured condition-consequence proposition to v 4. The artist then employs the identical stylistic stratagem in yet

another verse. V 5 is the third verse to begin with the word
*'ăzay,* "then." Each of these collocations direct the reader's at-
tention back to the two premises upon which the consequences
rest. The work turns in on itself. The artist presents a condition
(v 1), expands upon it (v 2), offers a consequence (v 3), a second
consequence (v 4), and a third consequence (v 5). Each line,
moreover, is externally signalled as part of the cause and conse-
quence chain by carrying the technical term "had it not
been. . ." or "then. . ./therefore." The psalmist progresses and
elaborates but at the same time recalls the overall structure,
subsuming each advancement in meaning under the same logi-
cal superstructure.

Let us look at the various depictions of the enemies of Israel
in Ps 124. The rapidly shifting images—a new one in almost
each successive verse is striking. The result is, however, not one
of kaleidoscopic variation as in Song of Songs 5:10-16, for exam-
ple. Amidst the shifts of image in Ps 124, the artist plays with
several threads that run through the complete set of likenesses.

One unifying thread is the selection of analogies for Israel's
enemies that represent the set of two cosmic realms—the two-
fold division into land and water (cf. Gen 1:9-10).

| v 2 | man (land) |
|-----|------------|
| v 3 | animals (land) |
| v 4 | water |
| v 5 | water |
| v 6 | animals (land) |

Thus, merismatically, the artist expresses that the totality of
creation is against Israel. This points all the more to YHWH's
greatness in His deliverance of Israel from such a formidable
alignment of adversaries.

Another unifying thread is the allusion to the set of
primordial enemies of YHWH and therefore of Israel, YHWH's
people. The "swallowing up alive" (v 3) and the "prey to their
teeth" (v 5) suggest mythical ravening beasts. The raging
waters and torrent (vv 4 and 5) are references to the chaotic
primeval sea.

V 6 invokes the name YHWH, echoing vv 1 and 2, and forms
an envelope figure around the triple announcement of what
could have befallen Israel had the Lord not been with/for Israel.
The YHWH echo and the framing figure draw the parts of the
work together. Then the psalmist returns to an earlier image.
By mentioning "prey to their teeth" in v 6, the psalmist evokes
the beasts of v 3.

No set of images in a poem is static. With each new image, the understanding of the set shifts. Poetry thrives on multiple conceptions of figures. What is understood as a hint of a primeval ravening beast swallowing its prey alive is also construed as the netherworld of Sheol that is never sated (cf. Exod 15:12; Num 16:30-33; Ps 106:17; Prov 1:12 and Hos 8:7). Whether taken as mythical animals or the yawning maws of the underworld, the congruence of metaphor is maintained by the complementary image of the torrential waters. Land and water represent the almost infinite range of enemies besetting Israel.

The psalmist suggests another conception of the set of images for the enemies of Israel by the adverbial phrase "when their anger was kindled against us" (v 3). Fire is an oft-used metaphor for anger. The particular collocation of this metaphor here enriches the work by conjuring up the set of primal elements: fire, land and water.

Varying similitudes here relate. The artist has suggested multiple links. The work, as a result, emerges as an interlocking whole rather than as an aggregate of unconnected metaphors. Each figure recalls and produces with the other metaphors a set that imparts a feeling of wholeness and totality.

V 7 presents new analogies that also mesh with the literary likenesses already expressed. The soul/life of Israel is here depicted as a bird escaping from the snare of fowlers. At first reading the bird seems to constitute another distinct artistic picture. The weakness and vulnerability of the bird is certainly an apt representation of the imperiled soul of Israel (cf. Lam 3:52). A deeper reflection on the integrated poem reveals a broadening of the organizing principle. The entire universe is the stage upon which the drama of Israel's peril and deliverance is enacted. Land and water comprise a dyadic conception of the cosmos. The introduction of the bird in v 7 modifies this conception into the threefold land, sea and air division or set (cf. the creation of the animals on the sixth day, after the birds and the fish had already been created on the fifth day in Gen 1:20-25).

Verse 8 provides a fine closure for the entire piece. A fourth explicit invocation of YHWH echoes vv 1 and 2. The final words of the psalm cap the poem thematically. The formulaic phrase "maker of heaven and earth" is most fitting here. The common merism expresses the universality of the Lord's creative powers and dominion. In Ps 124, the psalmist lauds YHWH's sovereignty over the totality of the cosmos. It is precisely this quality that has saving power against the cosmic dangers specified. The merism formula "maker of heaven and earth" is also a recognized epithet for YHWH (cf. 121:2 and 134:3). The poem thus opens with the words, "Had it not been *YHWH* that was with us. . ." and closes with, "Our help is in the name of *YHWH*, the maker of heaven and earth." This inclusio provides a satisfying structural and thematic closure to Ps 124.

The inclusio is not alone in contributing to the overall unity and tightness of the psalm. The artist organizes the work into a number of chiastic arrangements as well.

1) On the level of the whole:
   A  v 1  YHWH (=help)
      B  v 2  man (arising against us)
         C  v 3  animal (swallowing alive)
            D  v 4  water (carrying off)
            D'  v 5  water (sweeping over)
         C'  v 6  animal (prey to their teeth)
      B'  v 7  man (laying his snare)
   A'  v 8  YHWH (=help)

2) On the level of two consecutive verses:
   A   v 4  Then the *waters* would have carried us off. . .
   B   v 4  . . .Then the torrent would have *swept over us*
   B'  v 5  Then would have *swept over us*. . .
   A'  v 5  . . .the seething *waters*

3) On the level of the single verse (v 7):
   A   Our soul like a bird, *escaped*
   B   from the fowlers *snare*
   B'  the *snare* was broken
   A'  and we *escaped*

One further observation combines the concern for the set of Israel's adversaries and the psalmist's arrangement of the poem. The enemies are first depicted as human (v 2), then as animals (v 3) and thirdly as natural elements (= water). J. Trublet and J.-N Aletti perceptively point to an "anti-creation" presentation. The creatures ". . . revolt against YHWH's faithful instead of serving them. The series is not as in Gen 1, elements-animals-human, but the opposite: the original order is lost."[19]

---

[19] J. -N. Aletti and J. Trublet, *Approche poétique et théologique des psaumes* (Paris: Initiations, Editions du Cerf, 1983) 248-49.

The unifying elements are undeniably present in Ps 124. The structure is also ambivalent. Some of the compositional devices summon to mind these same and similar devices in other psalms which open and extend the text of the individual psalm.

A distinctive repetition scheme is apparent in the opening verses of the psalm. We have already discussed the reiteration of "Had it not been. . ." (vv 1, 2). The words that intervene between the appearance of this phrase are "let Israel say." It is noteworthy that Ps 129:1 also evidences a striking repetition of its first three words. More impressive and to the point is that the identical phrase, "let Israel say" separates the two occurrences of the phrase in 124:1 and 129:1. The same intervening phrase occurs in Ps 118:2 also.

The waters are hostile in Ps 130 as they are in Ps 124. The psalmist there calls to YHWH "from the depths" (cf. Ps 18:4, 16; 69:1, 2, 14, 15; 144:7 and 130:1).

The particular form *hazzēdōnīm* "seething" (v 5) is unique to Ps 124. Usually *zēd* is used. The usage of a less common or even rare form for a more conventional one is reminiscent of the use of *ṣārātāh* for *ṣārāh* (120:1), *'ōyāh* for *'ōy* (120:5), *rabbat* for *rabbāh* (120:7 and 1209:1, 2) and *'awlātāh* for *'awlāh* (125:3). The abundance of such forms led Dahood to write "pss cxx-cxxxiv teem with dialectal elements. . ." and suggest a common provenance.[20]

*Psalm 127*

This psalm deals with two themes. Some critical scholarship has even suggested that the psalm is made up of two independent works that were put together with no semantic development from one to the other.[21]

The first part, vv 1-2, is structured somewhat as Ps 124 is structured. There are two conditional sentences in v 1, each marked by the same rhetorical structure.

> *'im YHWH lō' . . . šāwě' . . .*
> If YHWH does not. . .in vain does [a person]. . .

The repetition of the identical logical framework keeps the work cohesive. The two propositions assert that mere human activity is of no avail as long as the Lord does not act in concert. The vain nature of the endeavors constitutes the common

20 Dahood, *Psalms III*, 196 and cf. 204.
21 Cf. Weiser, *The Psalms*, 777.

thread, both thematically and linguistically, running through v 1. V 2 begins with *šāwĕ'*, "in vain," the same word that appeared twice in v 1. The word *šāwĕ'*, "in vain" occurs three times in vv 1 and 2.

V 2 expresses three additional vain human activities. The five futile pursuits set forth are: toil at building a house, watchfulness at guarding a city, arising early, retiring late, and eating bread of toil. The psalmist states explicitly that "as long as YHWH is not building the house" and "as long as YHWH is not guarding the city" these two activities by a human alone are of no avail. In the case of the three remaining enterprises the condition is implicit but not stated. The reader advances in the reading but brings the conditional superstructure to bear.

The parallelistic pair of words "house" and "city" functions as a cohesive feature but moreover adds to the semantic development. The distinction between house and city is one of magnitude and domain. The poet effects a development from small and familial to large and communal by the progress from "house" (1a) to "city" (1c).

Vv 3-5 extol the blessing of many children as a divine gift and as protection and defense against enemies. The connection between vv 1-2 and vv 3-5 is not readily apparent. There are, however, remarkable ties. On the phonological level, the repeated sounds reverberate.[22] The play on the *b* sounds is noted in *yibneh bayit . . . bōnāyw bō* (127:5). The alliteration of *š* in *yišmōr . . . šāwĕ' šāqad šōmēr* (127:1) resounds in *'ašrēy . . . 'ašer . . . 'ašpātō*. The congruity in sound bridges the thematic gap.

On the stylistic level there is also an interlocking figure. Distant parallel members combine in the reader's perception of three oft-related words. The opening member, *bayit*, "house," (127:1a), is answered by *'īr*, "city" (127:1c). The two which frequently appear together (cf. 2 Kgs 10:5, Zech 14:2) are both recalled in the final word of the psalm, *ša'ar*, "gate." The recollection creates an inclusio. "Gate" is a conventional complement to "house" (cf. Deut 6:9; Deut 11:20). Ps. 122:1 and 2 also evidences the collocation of "house" and "gate." The three terms, "house," "city" and "gate" are all taken from the same semantic field and constitute an associative cluster. The three terms appear together in Neh 2:8.

The first chief element mentioned in 127:1 is "house." The theme of 127:3 is children as the gift of God and the fruit of the

---

[22] Dahood, *Psalms III*, 222-23.

womb as a reward. There is a close relationship between the blessedness and prosperity of the house and the children within or about it (cf. Ps 128). There is also a close connection between children and builders. The Talmud recognizes this affinity as well as the paronomastic ties in its comment, "Do not read 'your children' (*bānayik*) but rather 'your builders' (*bōnayik*)!"[23] The second proposition propounded in 127:1 relates to the city. Vv 4-5 assert the likeness of children to the "arrows of a warrior" and the children's ability to meet the enemy at the "gate." Ps 127 argues that under YHWH's providence house and city are blessed with children and protectors.

The tenuous connection does lead some contemporary scholars to divide the psalm. A careful analysis of centripetality is not only to be sought, however, in obvious narrative logic. Ps 127 evidences abundant means whereby poetic works achieve balance between looseness and tightness of composition. Therefore, splitting the psalm is not necessary.

### Psalm 128

Psalm 128 commends the reader to fear the Lord and walk in His ways for such a one is blessed and happy (v 1). In vv 2-6, the psalmist assures that domestic happiness will be the reward. A change in grammatical person that occurs in v 2 underscores the emblematic nature of v 1. V 1 is objective, general in its third person announcement. The ensuing verses are personal and specific in their second person apostrophe to the faithful one. A similar shift in person occurs in Ps 127:1-2. "To walk in His ways" is a typically graphic mode of expression preferred to the abstract profession of faith. The antithesis of this behavior is set down in Ps 125:5, "those turning aside [in] their crooked [ways] YHWH will lead them [in the way of] evildoers." Ps 128:2-6 enumerates the blessings that the faithful one of 128:1 will enjoy: "The labor of your hands" is to be understood as the fruits of that labor. This Hebrew mode of expression is analogous to *ḥeṭēʾ* meaning commonly "sin" but also the consequence of sin, i.e., "punishment" (cf. Lev 20:20; 24:15; Num 9:13; 18:32). *kī* is an emphatic particle. I therefore render v 2:

> The fruits of your toil you shall surely eat;
> Happy you [shall be] and it will be well with you.

---

[23] At the end of *Ber.*, in commentary on Isa 54:13.

V 3 presents us with two carefully structured parallel lines that advance the blessing begun in v 2.

> Your wife [will be] like a fruitful vine
> in the innermost parts of your house;
> Your children [will be] like olive plantings
> around your table.

By casting a list into a designed progression. The psalmist makes the items hang together. Each recalls the former and anticipates the following. The entirety is draw together. There is a progression here from "well with *you*" (v 2) to "your wife" (v 3a), to "your children" (3b). The sequence from the closest to the less close reflects a psychological reality—the gradation in the levels of intimacy: 1) the man (himself), 2) his wife, and 3) his children. The progression unifies the aspects of the blessing, making the discrete parts an organic whole.

The poet expresses the blessedness of the wife and the children through similes: she is likened to a fruitful vine and they to olive plantings. The fecund quality and perhaps also the clinging dependent nature of the vine make the analogy to the wife a felicitous one. The care in choice of the "vine" as a simile for the wife is apt also on account of the gender matching of the vehicle and the tenor. *gepen*, "vine," is a feminine noun as is obviously *'iššāh*, "wife." The psalmist makes an equally fitting selection in creating the second simile for children. Olive plantings are used as similes of beauty (Hos 14:7) and prosperity (Ps 52:10). The vehicle in this likeness also matches its tenor in gender and number—*šĕtiley zēytīm*, "olive plantings," is masculine plural and matches *bānīm*, "children."

As in the other Songs of Ascents, the artist of Ps 128 delimits the range of the psalm to the domestic scene. The semantic field from which the imagery is drawn is confined to the everyday life within the compass of the family and home.

The adverbial spatial phrases of each line comport well structurally and thematically. They direct the attention of the reader to the two major areas of the domestic milieu. The poet situates the wife *bĕyarkĕtēy bēytekā* "in the innermost parts of your house." The home was certainly the primary locus of the woman. The prepositional phrase "in the innermost parts of," however, demands comment. *yarkĕtēy* means "innermost parts," "recesses" in the sense of the inner angle where the two sides or walls meet. Thus, for example, it signifies the interior of a ship (Jonah 1:5), i.e., the point where its flanks meet; or the

inside of a cave where its sides meet (1 Sam 24:4); or of a valley
(Judg 19:1). Deriving from *yĕrēkayim*, "the two thighs,"
*yarkĕtēy* applies to a bifurcation (cf. Exod 26:23). This
etymology summons to mind another association. Ps 128:3 cites
"your wife" immediately referring to her fecundity in the simile
"like a fruitful vine." I propose that the psalmist extended the
concept of fruitfulness by use of a particularly congruent term,
*yarkĕtēy*, suggesting thighs, loins, generative organs (cf. Gen
46:26; Judg 30:8). The blessing of procreation is featured in the
evocation of the woman and in the phrase relative to her.

In regard to the children, the psalmist compares them to
olive plantings *"around your table."* This juxtaposition of
children, olive plantings and the table recalls "the *fruit* of your
toil you shall surely *eat*" (v 2). The coherence of imagery raises
an ambivalence in the reader's mind. Is the scene of the faithful
man eating the fruit of his toil a figurative or literal depiction?
Indeed, the real and rhetorical merge. The children *are* about
the festal table at which all are partaking of the fruits of their
labor. The Hebrew term *sābīb*, "around," is the same as that
used in Ps 125:2: *yĕrūšālēm hārīm sābīb lāh*, "Jerusalem,
mountains about it," and *wĕYHWH sābīb lĕʿammō*, "and YHWH
is around His people." The inter-psalm allusion clarifies the
semantic plane by introducing God's protectiveness from Ps 125
and also brings in a centrifugal force that tends away from the
psalm at hand by referring to an extratextual item.

The variation of the two prepositional phrases, "in the
innermost parts," i.e., "deep within," (relating to the wife) and
"around," "about" (relating to the children) seems to have been
chosen to intimate encompassment of the *entire* domestic
scene—within and without.

With v 4 the psalmist returns to the third person description:

> Behold, surely thus shall be blessed, a man fearing
> YHWH (v 4)

The grammatical person, the explicit rehearsal of the words,
*yĕrē ʾYHWH*, "fearing YHWH," and the word *yĕbōrak*, "shall-be-
blessed," paralleling *ʾašrēy*, "happy-is," (= "blessed is") all serve
to recall v 1 and create with it a neat frame for the picture of the
blessed household in vv 2-3.

Vv 5-6 now broaden the scope of the psalm and place the
blessing in a wider, national context. The poet already inti-
mated this broadening of focus by suggesting subtly that "chil-

dren *around* your table" are analogous to "mountains about Jerusalem."

> May YHWH bless you from Zion (v 5a)

Although the focus is greatly enlarged, from the individual to the national, the cohesiveness of the two fields is maintained. The poet reverts back to the second person of vv 2-3, creating an alternating pattern of grammatical person:

| | |
|---|---|
| v 1 | third person singular |
| vv 2-3 | second person singular |
| v 4 | third person singular |
| vv 5-6a | second person singular |

Moreover, two words appearing in v 4 are repeated in v 5. One is in a different form and the other fulfills a different syntactic function. V 4, *yĕbōrak*, "shall-be-blessed," retains its four consonants but becomes *yĕbārekĕkā*, "he-will-bless-you," in v 5. The different form of *brk* and the different syntactic function of YHWH do not break the continuity. The phonetic properties of their first mention resonate in the second.

| | |
|---|---|
| 5b | and see the prosperity of Jerusalem |
| 5c | all the days of your life! |
| 6a | and see children to your children |
| 6b | peace upon Israel! |

These final two parallel bicola integrate the broader and narrower foci of the psalm. "The prosperity of Jerusalem" (5b) finds its echo in "children to your children." Children are the beauty and prosperity of the family as indicated by the simile "like olive plantings." "Prosperity" and "children" are linked.

The psalmist links the opening and closing lines also by paronomastic means. V 1 *yĕrē'*, "fearing," resounds in the phonetically close *rĕ'ēh*, "see!" of vv 5-6. The assonantal envelope figure delimits the psalm, YHWH bringing the reader back to the point of origin. The phrases "all the days of your life" (v 5) and "peace upon Israel" (v 6) also correspond parallelistically. Together, they evoke the temporal and spatial dimensions. The longevity of the faithful father seeing children to his children is recalled in the temporal "all the days of your life" (v 5). The extension of scope of the home to the entire nation resonates in the formulaic spatial blessing "[May] peace [be] upon Israel" (v 6).

The tightly woven fabric of the psalm opens with a general

statement of blessing (v 1) which is made specific in familial terms (vv 2-3) and summarized in v 4. Vv 5-6 extend the blessing and transcend the particular family. The structure of the work makes it clear that the entire people of Zion (5a), Jerusalem (5b) and Israel (6) are to be blessed along with the faithful man (v 1), his wife (v 3a) and his children (3c). The parallelism indicates that prosperity and longevity are assured equally to the home and to the nation, and peace will abide upon both. Sound complements theme in the assonance of *šālōm*, "peace," *šulḥān*, "table," and *yĕrūšālēm*, "Jerusalem". The correspondence of sound links the already related thematically pregnant terms.

## Psalm 131

This is a very brief psalm of three neatly structured verses. The psalmist first turns to YHWH asserting the psalmist's humility and meekness (v 1). In v 2a the psalmist suggests that it was not always this way, and in 2b and c the artist offers an analogy to the current state of equanimity. In v 3 the psalmist calls upon Israel to place their hope in YHWH forever. V 1 is the longest verse of the three. It comprises four parallel cola all cast in the negative:

> O Lord, my heart is not haughty;
> my eyes are not raised high.
> I do not walk to and fro (= occupy myself)
>     with great [matters]
> [nor] with wonders beyond me.

The fourfold disavowal of any pride indicates, by its abundant denials, a familiarity with pride. The next verse, by beginning with

> I surely have smoothed and quieted my soul (v 2ab).

intimates that once the psalmist was indeed intimate with the loftiness that is now controlled and tempered.

In the four lines of v 1, the arrogance is suggested by the explicit postures of haughtiness that are denied. Having listed the specific sins, the psalmist conveys a message. The fact of disclaiming participation in these postures does not succeed in erasing them. The psalmist smoothes and quiets the haughty stirrings of the soul (v 2a) allowing for the submissiveness and dependence, expressed in the two similes of the infant, to reign

> . . .like an infant [resting] on his mother
> like an infant on me is my soul (v 2 b-c).

It is noteworthy that the echoing in these lines is heard not only in the word *kĕgāmūl*, "like an infant," but also in the preposition that follows. Although in English "on" in "on his mother" and "on me" is identical, in Hebrew the former is *ălēy* and the latter *ālay*. Nevertheless, the two are sufficiently alike to answer one another. Consonantally they are identical.

The word translated "infant," *gāmūl*, is properly "weaned" or "a weaned one." Weiser takes this word in its literal meaning and comments, ". . . not like an infant crying loudly for his mother's breast, but like a weaned child. . . . just as the child gradually breaks off the habit of regarding his mother only as a means of satisfying his own desires and learns to love her for her own sake, so the worshipper. . . . He now rests no longer in himself but in God."[24] The metaphor, as Weiser explains it, is a powerful vehicle for transmitting the message of the psalmist. The analogy coheres eminently with the entire theme of the work.

The final lines of the poem exude the fullest sense of profound piety and serenity.

> Hope, O Israel, in YHWH
> Now and forever (v 3)

The progress of the psalmist's soul from loftiness to profundity is reflected in the structure of the verses. The longest verse (4 cola), with the shifting images of "haughty heart," "raised eyes," "walking to and fro" and the "great and wondrous," gives rise to the shorter three-cola v 2 with more controlled lines. Here the psalmist smoothes and quiets the exercised soul projecting a tranquility in the two analogies of the infant. The psalm draws to a close in the shortest of the verses with the formulaic utterance "now and forever" (cf. 121:8). The conventional term offers a sense of security, permanence and stability. The progressive shortening of verses serves to convey movement from plurality, deviation and individuality to uniformity, constancy and community.

The poem opens with the vocative "YHWH" and closes with the vocative "Israel" in an exhortation to place hope in YHWH. The syntactic inclusio of vocatives suggests the progress from a

---

24 Weiser, *The Psalms*, 777.

personal, intimate experience to a lesson learned and now taught to all Israel.

The verb forms show the movement also. V 1 displays three verbs in the perfect signifying a remote past. V 2a shows two verbs in the perfect—a less remote past. V 2 b and c exhibit two participles—the present state. V 3 reveals one jussive verb—a projection into the future. The odyssey of the soul is told by the psalmist. The lexical, grammatical, structural and figurative elements selected determine the nature of that telling and the nature of that odyssey.

## THE COLLECTION AS A WHOLE

The internal structure of the several Songs of Ascents is generally centered in on itself. That is not to say that there are no centrifugal forces, but the predominant compositional form of the individual psalms is more centripetally oriented. Is there an overall organization of the fifteen psalms into an integral whole which complements the integrality of each discrete smaller unit? On the level above that of the single psalm, are there forces striving toward a unity? The complex of elements is not easy to sort out. There are contradictory tugs and pulls. The fifteen units—each whole in and of itself—are collocated to one another. Each also bears the same title. To borrow terms from Roman Jakobson, we now turn from mere "contiguity" and seek "equivalence."

### Linguistic Peculiarities

There are strange language uses that appear to an inordinate degree in Pss 120-134 which distinguish the collection from other bodies of poetry. The strange linguistic elements in these psalms lend to them a dynamic double motion common in much poetry. The commonality of the peculiarities tie the psalms together and the exotic character of each oddity foregrounds the part at the expense of the whole. Numerous anomalies and rare forms figure in the collection. Evode Beaucamp identifies many of these words within the fifteen psalms.[25] I owe much to Beaucamp's work in the present section.

The number of odd words is impressive when we recall that these psalms are, by and large, marked by extreme brevity. Ps 132 with its eighteen verses is the only one of the fifteen with more than nine verses. The following words do not display un-

[25] E. Beaucamp, "L'Unité du Recueil des Montées: Psaumes 120-1394," *Liber annuus Stadium Biblicum Franciscanum* 29 (1979) 73-90.

known and unattested stems but rather a form and/or spelling
that is strange to biblical Hebrew.

| 122:3 | *šeḥubbĕrāh lāh* |
| 123:4 | *ša'ănannīm* |
| 124:3, 5 | *'ăzay* |
| 124:5 | *zēydōnīm* |
| 126:1 | *šibat* |
| 126:6 | *mešek* |
| 127:2 | *šēnā'* |
| 128:3 | *šĕtilēy* |
| 129:1, 2 | *ṣĕrārūnī* |
| 129:3 | *ma'ănwt* |
| 129:6 | *šeqadmat* |
| 129:7 | *mĕ'ammēr* |
| 130:4 | *hassĕliḥāh* |

The linguistic peculiarities of our small collection are not
limited to spelling and formal oddities. Some terms more
familiar to classical biblical literature are as odd as the formal
rarities due to the striking contexts into which they are placed.
The number of uncommon phrases is a fair warning against too
facile a recourse to emendation. Some of these phrases I treat in
my explication of individual psalms. Here, I just note the
strangeness of the following locutions: Ps 132:17, *'aṣmīāḥ*
relating to *qeren*; Ps 132:18, *yāṣīṣ* relating to *nezer*; Ps 130:3, *šmr*
and 130:8 *pdh* used with *ăwōnōt*; Ps 125:1, *yṣb* and 132:13 *'wh*
relative to "Jerusalem" with "YHWH" as subject. A unique
expression in the Bible is Ps 122:4 *šibṭēy yāh*.[26]

Pss 120-134 constitute but ten percent of psalms in the
Psalter; the one hundred one verses comprise only four percent
of the total number of verses in Psalms. Several particles are
used in the Songs of Ascents over and above their proportional
use in the rest of Psalms or the entire Scriptures: *hinnēh* (Pss
121:4; 123:2; 127:3; 128:4; 132:6; 133:1; 134:1) appears seven
times in these psalms, more than twenty-five percent of the
total occurrences in all one hundred fifty psalms. Twenty-five
percent of the occurrences of the particle *kēn* in the Psalter are
concentrated in Pss 120-134. *Rabbat* appears four times in this
collection out of a total of seven times in the entire Hebrew
Bible. *'im lō'* also serves to make the language of these psalms
stand out. The abbreviated relative pronoun *še-* (Pss 122:4;
123:2; 124:1, 2, 6; 129:6, 7; 133:2, 3) in preference to the
standard form *'ăšer* (Pss 127:5; 132:2) further marks this

26 Beaucamp, "L'Unité," 75.

collection. The Song of Songs, however, is the only biblical book that uses the relative particle *še-* consistently throughout the book. There is one use of the standard particle *'ăšer*, but that is in the superscription to the Song of Songs. In the Songs of Ascents, the uncommonly high frequency of the *še-* is also noteworthy. One further peculiarity of locution is the employment of *šām*, "there," to designate Jerusalem (Pss 122:4, 5; 132:17; 133:3).

The concentration of these unconventional language features in Pss 120-139⁴ imparts to the group a special texture and noteworthy quality. The commonality draws the individuals together. The sharing imparts a centripetality.

*Transtextuality*

The integrity of the individual psalms is complemented by an overall organization of the parts into an organic whole. Common linguistic features across psalm boundaries, the shared superscription, recurrent words, the characteristic brevity and limited thematic compass are some of the external integrating features. Leon J. Liebreich related the entire collection of the Songs of Ascents to a text outside of the small collection and even outside of the entire Psalter.[27] Particular importance attaches to this brief study. Liebreich claims that the extratextual allusion is the key to the Songs of Ascents. The affinities between Pss 120-134 and Num 6:24-26, Liebreich claims, can account for the repetition of key words, the connection to Zion and Jerusalem, the basis of inclusion of all fifteen psalms, the explanation of the specific number "fifteen," the early application of these psalms and the meaning of the title.

Twelve of the psalms (120, 121, 122, 123, 125, 127, 128, 129, 130, 132., 133, 134) directly evoke four key words in the Priestly Benediction: *yĕbārekĕkā*, "may He [YHWH] bless you," *wĕyiš-mĕrekā*, "and may He protect you," *wiyḥunnekk ā*, "and may He be gracious to you," and *šālōm*, "peace."

The starting point of the Songs of Ascents is a verbal association with the Priestly Blessing of Num 6:24-26. The psalms proceed from this to a thematic elaboration of the laconic style of the Blessing. The opening words of the Blessing demonstrate the verbal tie and semantic expansion developed in Pss 120-134. I briefly trace these associations by way of example:

*yĕbārekĕkā YHWH*, "may YHWH bless you" (Num 6:24) is

[27] L. J. Liebreich, "The Songs of Ascents and the Priestly Blessing" *JBL* 74 (1955) 33-36.

understood as emanating from Zion (128:5; 133:3; 134:3). Zion is where YHWH chose his abode (132:13-14). Jerusalem is the site of the Temple (122:1; 132:7), the site of the Ark (132:8), the sphere of the priests (132:9, 16). Those who put their faith in YHWH are likened to Mount Zion (125:1). The enemies of Zion will be thwarted shamefully (129:5). Although Ps 126 does not have an explicit verbal association with the Benediction, it is included in the psalm collection on account of its theme of the restoration of the fortune of Zion. Zion is repeatedly associated with the Lord's blessing. The blessing is realized in life (133:3), provisions (132:15), home, family and children (128:3-4, 6, and 127:3-5).

Thus, a repetition of the key word signals an expansion of that concept. Although I have explained the elaboration of only the opening words of the Blessing, Liebreich traces the verbal/thematic plays on each of the four key words. The echoes of the four key words explain the inclusion of twelve of the Songs of Ascents. The three psalms (124, 126 and 131) that do not have a direct verbal relationship to the Priestly Benediction show indirect associations. Again, I use the opening words of the Blessing, "may YHWH bless you," as an instructive example of the associative projections of all four key words into the Songs of Ascents. The insistent linking of Zion with the Benediction warranted the embracing of Ps 126 as one of the Songs of Ascents despite the absence of an explicit reference to the Benediction in Ps 126. The theme of Ps 126 is the restoration of the fortune of Zion. The need was felt to raise the total number of psalms in the collection from twelve to fifteen to correspond to the fifteen words in the Priestly Blessing. Thus, psalms only indirectly related to the Blessing, by way of "Zion" and other aspects of the Blessing were incorporated into the Songs of Ascents also.

Liebreich's Priestly Benediction connection can also elucidate the significance of the superscription of these psalms. The Blessing in Num 6:24-26 was recited by the priests on the steps (ma'ălōt) of the hall leading to the interior of the Temple.[28] The title, šīr hamma'ălōt, therefore, can connote a song sung on "the steps" (of the hall). Each song, the theory goes, was a response to the Priestly Blessing. The recital of the Priestly Blessing in the Jewish synagogue service preserves a custom akin to Liebreich's proposed elaboration of the Benediction by the Songs of Ascents. After each word of the Blessing chanted by

[28] Tosephta Sota VVI 7.

the descendants of the priests, a response is offered of a scriptural verse containing that word. Another analogy in the Jewish liturgy is the recitation of the *śīm šālōm* prayer of the *amidah* directly following the Priestly Blessing which concludes with the word *šālōm*. The *śīm šālōm* prayer contains references to the other parts of the Benediction, as well.

The underlying, subtextual, implicit dimension of the Songs of Ascents consequently rests in the collection being an elaboration on key words in the Priestly Blessing. We thus recognize a double motion, toward and away from a central orientation. The text is expanded, the whole now includes the transtextual reference which modifies the narrower text. The whole qualifies the meaning of the parts, while the parts are gathered and contribute to the meaning of the whole. The Psalms of Ascents resound with echoes of a different literature. The transtextuality complicates the reading, makes the comprehension of its meaning more complex, and diverts the pursuance of a hypothetical central message. Paradoxically, the recognition of an extratextual referent simultaneously lends focus to the work, exposing what was hitherto veiled and providing the necessary means for decoding of the text, albeit only one new dimension thereof.[29] The art of the poem emerges in shifting perspectives and an unsteady equilibrium between openness and closedness, between centrifugal and centripetal pulls.

## Narrative Development

Expositors throughout the generations have attempted to join the individual psalms into an elusive coherent whole marked by internal development. They claim the thread on which the fifteen psalms are strung is a pilgrimage to Jerusalem. A representative exposition of this type follows.[30]

---

[29] Robert Alter raises a related issue in regard to transtextuality: "The Hebrew Bible, because it so frequently articulates its meanings by recasting texts within its own corpus, is already moving toward being an integrated work for all its anthological diversity" and "Intertextual play occurs repeatedly in the Hebrew Bible, drawing its disparate elements into a certain mobile, unpredictable unity ("Introduction to the Old Testament" in *The Literary Guide to the Bible*, R. Alter and F. Kermode, eds. (Caambridge: The Belknap Press of Harvard University Press, 1987) 13, 14.

[30] Neale and Littledale, *A Commentary*, 115. Cf. M. Mannati, "Les psaumes graduels constitutent-ils un genre littéraire distinct à l'intérieur du psautier biblique?" *Sem* 29 (1979) 85-100.

120 expresses weariness of pagan environment.
121 the first glimpse of the mountains of Israel by the
     pilgrim who trusts in YHWH to protect him on
     his journey.
122 the convergence of pilgrims as they approach the
     approach to Jerusalem.
123 a prayer uttered in a state of fear from attack by
     bandits.
124 thanksgiving for deliverance from that peril.
125 the first sight of the Judean hills around Jerusalem.
126 happy and peaceful talk between pilgrims and
     their hosts offering food and shelter.
127 in sight of the peaceful city, a recollection of past
     war brought on by neglect of the true builder of
     the glorious House and the one sure watchman
     of its wall.
128 greeting to the citizens of Jerusalem who come out
     meet them.
129 grateful expression of security by pilgrims who are
     now within the walls.
130 in view of the Temple, an expression of primitive
     longing and hope from the valley "depths" as
     they prepare to ascend Mt. Moriah.
131 the hush of reverence as they approach YHWH's
     house.
132 in full view of the beauty of the Temple, the
     pilgrims break into praise and blessing and recall
     David's zeal for the Tabernacle.
133 emotional outburst at sight of the priests on the
     steps and in the outer court.
134 within the sacred precincts, the greeting to the
     priests whom they had seen at a little distance
     just before. The closing words of Ps 134 carry a
     blessing of the travelers by the Temple priests.

The final blessing by the priests is an appropriate end to the
pilgrimage and to the entire small Pilgrim Psalter. It constitutes
a kind of inclusio, being a final reply to the first utterance of the
series, "Unto YHWH, in my straits I call" (120:1). The answer is,
"May YHWH bless you out of Zion, the maker of heaven and
earth" (134:3).

The scanty textual support for the detailed outline of
development proposed here has prevented its fuller
acceptance. Certainly, several of the psalms can sustain such an
interpretation; others have been made to fit with but the least
evidence. We have here a pious motivation born of reverence
for Scripture and particular organizational principles imputed

to it.  This motivation joins with a reader's natural search for significance and connection in the juxtaposition of any texts. The anticipation itself and its complementary fulfillment or the anticipation of significance and linkage and the frustration of the anticipation, constitute tension in the constant review necessary for the apprehension of the poetic work. The centeredness and outward tendency are at one and the same time conjuncts of the constantly reassessing form of reading.

Evode Beaucamp analyzes the collection and discerns a different logical order in the psalms.[31]  The initial cry in 120 to the utterance of the blessing in 134 provides the avenue or progress.  There is a threefold recurrence of the ascent from anguish to total confidence in YHWH: Pss 120-122, 123-128, and 129-134. Jerusalem figures prominently in the three.  In the first, one goes up towards the city; in the second, one enjoys its security; and in the third, one draws from it guarantees for the future.  Indeed, each of the three stages does evidence the respective posture posited for it.  Selective vision makes the design more compelling than a more critical study does. Beaucamp deserves recognition for the careful study of linguistic and literary factors in this collection that mark it as a unity.  The attempt to reveal an elaborate logical internal order falters, however.  A thoroughgoing convincing scheme is elusive here, just as it is in Song of Songs.

The suggestion of logical development in the text imparts a tightness and connectedness of the parts.  The very fact of the division into the several parts is an atomizing and fragmentary force.  The tension between the two tendencies is the essence of the art form.

---

[31] Beaucamp, "L'Unité," 86-90.

# CHAPTER 2

# SONG OF SONGS

A review of the interpretations of Song of Songs reveals several primary avenues of access to the meaning of the work. The allegorical, cult-mythological, and naturalistic are those that have gained widest acceptance. Each approach rose to prominence (although never winning scholarly unanimity) and subsequently lost ground to a rival view.

The differing understandings of the meaning and intent of the book are complemented by a similar array of explanations of the structure and form of the Song. On the surface the book consists of a number of small units of love poetry. The different structural construings are traced to the answer given the following question: Is the book to be regarded as a single whole, into which all the units fit, or as an anthology of discrete poems? This chapter will contribute to the understanding of the contradictory answers proffered, by locating the compositional form of Song of Songs near the centrifugal extreme on the structural continuum.[1]

Song of Songs shares with Psalms and Lamentations the distinction of being entirely comprised of poetry (Proverbs and the Dialogue in Job are also entirely poetical). The structural forms of Psalms, Song of Songs and Lamentations, however, are as different from one another as are their general themes. Song of Songs deals with the mutual love and attraction of a man and woman; Psalms consists of reflections upon disparate aspects of God's revelation and diverse human responses to the revelations; Lamentations is a series of five elegies on destroyed Jerusalem. Notwithstanding the single unitary theme of the brief Song of Songs, the work is one whose dominant emphasis is on its parts.

Our identification of an array of compositional features in the Song leads us to fix its structural character nearer to the

---

[1] See D. Grossberg, "A Centrifugal Structure in Biblical Poetry," *Semiotica* 58 (1986) 139-150, for a brief presentation of some aspects set forth in the current chapter.

centrifugal extreme of the continuum with strong balancing centripetal features.

## PECULIAR AND EXOTIC ELEMENTS

Song of Songs is in many ways unique in the Bible. Several of its peculiar features impart a strangeness and exoticism not met with elsewhere in Scripture. Its elaborate imagery with exuberant metaphors drawn from nature pervade the text. The artists of Psalms and other biblical poetry dispersed throughout the Bible contemplate the elements of nature and natural phenomena with a poetic *and* religious eye. Nature is the immense arena in which God manifests his power and providence. The contemplation breaks forth into praise. In Song of Songs, as in no other biblical book, nature is evoked, appreciated, indeed exulted in, for its own sake. "Nature" is intended here in its broad sense, encompassing the geographical sphere in which proper names of lands, places, and cities abound; the topographical, in which different qualities of mountains, valleys, open fields and cultivated orchards are enumerated; the meteorological order affecting climate, rhythm of life, and its cycles; the inanimate realm of rocks and minerals; vegetation including trees, plants, flowers, and herbs; the domesticated and wild animal kingdom; and natural food and drink. All these elements command a prominent position in the Song.

There is hardly a region in the entire geographical sphere of the Songs that is not represented. The profusion of sites alluded to creates an elusive geographical background—sometimes Judean, sometimes Israelite, or Transjordanian, or Syrian or Egyptian. As such it shares a characteristic of wisdom literature: more Syro-Palestinian than Hebraic. It has a wider range than just the Hebrew people. Indeed the narrow, traditional, peculiarly Israelite concerns of other biblical works are absent. There is no mention of God in the entire work.[2] There are no ostensible theological, religious or moralistic intentions in this strangely secular work.

The exoticism arises also from the lexicon of the Song. It has more *hapax legomena* than any other biblical work (49 in 117 verses) and also more unusual words (at least 70).[3] This strange vocabulary, all its own, imparts a foreignness as does its unusual

[2] The final syllable -*yah* on the *šalhebetyāh* (8:6) is best understood as an indicator of the superlative, hence "a most vehement flame" and not "a flame of YHWH."
[3] T. J. Meek, "The Song of Songs: Introduction and Exegesis," *IB* 5 (New York and Nashville: Abingdon Press, 1956) 92.

syntactic conventions: widespread replacement of masculine for feminine pronouns, verbs and suffixes; the pleonastic use of the personal pronoun with the finite verb; and the employment of the anticipatory suffix followed by the relative particle and the possessive $l$.[4] The Song is also the only biblical book that uses the relative particle *še-* consistently throughout the book.[5]

We may thus see in Song of Songs aspects of two correlated tendencies common to poetry in the modern world, viz., the search for new poetic forms and the manipulation of language as a source of new poetic expression. The innovations in the use of linguistic forms and in general the experiments with language "have lent strength to the centrifugal tendencies of modern verse."[6]

At the same time that the unconventional imparts a centrifugal force, the balancing centripetal tendency arises. The very plethora of exotica in the Song creates a uniformity. One finds oneself totally surrounded by the striking and excitingly unusual. The widespread and constantly encountered foreign elements create an exotic world that paradoxically becomes familiar, centered and standard. The persistent recurrence of the alien does not defy categorization. On the contrary, its frequency enables the reader to process it. Rather than flying apart, the oddities group themselves and align themselves together. The abundance of centrifugal elements anomalously invests Song of Songs with a centripetality. The peculiar and the exotic are both atomizing and centralizing. A poetic tension is the result.

## ANTITELEOLOGICAL STRUCTURE

As in Lamentations and in many of the psalms in the Psalter, a clear division into lines and strophes, particularly when marked by acrostic patterning, or the use of refrains, creates a unifying structure. Poems with patent thematic design and goal-oriented development subordinate the parts. In Song of Songs, the units seek the status of wholes and the whole assumes the condition of a part. The teleological development in many psalms is in great contrast to the movement in multiple directions in the Song. The switching fields of reference (e.g., from animal, to architectural, to vegetable realms) produces a rich

---

[4] Ibid., 92.

[5] There is a single use of the relative particle *'ăšer* in the superscription.

[6] E. Stankiewicz, "Centripetal and Centrifugal Structures in Poetry," *Semiotica* 38 (1982) 234.

polychromatic effect that resists subsumption under one rubric or position in an ordered progression. The prominent focus of the Song is on the minute segments of the work. Any broad design is barely recognizable. The lovers are merely reveling in each other's company and attention.

Roland E. Murphy asserts:

> There is hardly any evidence of deliberate division by he editors. Despite some refrains (e.g., 2:7; 3:5; and 8:4), commentators differ widely in enumerating the poetic units. . . . It is probable that *Canticles* is, in fact a collection of love poems. . . . From what has been said it is clear that *Canticles* cannot be broken down to any meaningful outline.[7]

Theodore M. Robinson is even more outspoken in his advocacy of a "collection" interpretation of Song of Songs:

> The plain fact is that any attempt to find a consistent thread running through this book . . . must depend to a large extent on imaginative conjecture. All we can say for certain is that we have a collection of erotic lyrics, most of them short and some mutilated—in a few instances we seem to have only a single line.[8]

The foregoing view that the Song is an aggregate or anthology of discrete poems which have little or no unity represents one of the two major opposing positions defined in critical scholarship in regard to the structure.

The rival view maintains that Song of Songs is a *unity* of a number of short poems. There lacks any consensus among the adherents to the unity position regarding the nature of the unity. Many advance the notion that the Song is a love drama (Pouget and Guitton, Waterman, *et al.*), others, that it is a consistent and advancing representation of love from its budding through engagement and marriage to married life (Thilo) or a depiction of the progress from admiration of the beloved to union (Buzy). Each of these explanations of the literary form encounters difficulties. The entire absence of stage directions and of indications of speakers or change of speakers is one compositional objection to the drama or dialogue hypothesis. An im-

---

[7] R. E. Murphy, "Canticle of Canticles," *JBC*, R. E. Brown, J. A. Fitzmyer and R. E. Murphy, eds. (Englewood Cliffs, N.J.: Prentice-Hall, 1968) 506-7. Murphy modified this view in later studies; cf. "The Unity of the Song of Songs" *VT* 29 (1979) 436-43.

[8] T. M. Robinson, *The Poetry of the Old Testament* (London: Gerald Duckworth and Co., 1957) 199.

portant grammatical factor of Hebrew does often give us the possibility of determining whether a segment is addressed to a man or woman by distinguishing between the masculine and feminine of the second person pronouns and of the verb forms. In a like manner, the sex of the speaker is often fixed and from time to time we distinguish language put in the mouth of a group of people, though it is not always clear whether they are male or female.

The numerous proposals of diverse dramatic schemes is a compelling indication of how tenuous the hypothesis of the dramatic literary form is. There is no universal agreement or even near consensus on any of the following: the number of scenes; where they begin and end; the identification of the *dramatis personae*; their number; the demonstration of meaningful, continuous action; the outline of progress toward a goal; or the resolution of the inconsistencies in description of the young woman—first, as a country girl, then, as a city dweller.

Stankiewicz could well have used his description of modern poetry to depict Song of Songs: ". . . diffusion of content and direction is achieved by the suppression of place, time, and order of events. . ."[9] Narrative plot and culminating thrust are virtually nonexistent. This diffuseness further marks the centrifugal tendency of Song of Songs.

## Polyphony of Voices

Our discussion of the dramatic form included reference to the rapidly shifting scenes and speakers which make difficult the fixing of a consistent progress in the work. The fact of the several changing speakers in the Song of Songs itself is a centrifugal feature. The all-pervasive "I" (or "we") that tightens the text of Psalms and much of Lamentations is absent in Song of Songs. William Pouget and Jean Guitton identified twelve scenes in the Song marked by speeches made by all of the following: the Shulamite maiden, the beloved, his companions, Solomon, and the daughters of Jerusalem.[10] Samuel Sandmel, too, discovers several speakers. He even discerns a line inserted into a speech of the bride by a commentator.[11] The polyphony of voices diffuses the text by multiplying the points of view, and shifting the place. The many voices serve to expand the boundaries of the

9 Stankiewicz, "Centripetal," 228.
10 W. Pouget and J. Guitton, *Canticle of Canticles* (Nw York: Declan X, McMullen, 1948) 53-59.
11 S. Sandmel, *The Hebrew Scriptures: An Introduction to Their Literature and Religious Ideas* (New York: Oxford University Press, 1963) 315.

text, add diversity of content and contribute to the open-endedness of the composition.

## Abrupt Shifts

The repeated shifting of speakers is one of the kaleidoscopic changes occurring in the Song of Songs. Abrupt transitions of several types are present in the Song. In the next section I discuss the fleeting impression given by the images, each dazzling, and appearing in quick succession. At this point I note the shift in grammatical person, most evident in 1:2. The personal pronouns here present an incongruent progression: ". . . him . . . me . . . his . . . your . . . ." *Enallage,* the substitution of one grammatical form for another, e.g., of singular for plural, of present for past or as here of one grammatical person for another is an attested device in biblical poetry (cf. Deut 32:15; Isa 1:29; Jer 22:24; Micah 7:19). There is thus no need to emend the text to remove lack of agreement. The transitions are made unexpectedly, bringing with them juxtapositions of unrelated utterances, a dispersion and a staccato treatment of themes that disturbs a linear succession. Chap. 1:2-5 provides us with a rich sampling of sudden jumps of several kinds: of person (1:2), of speaker (1:4, 5), of addressee (1:4, 5), of sense domains (throughout), and of scene (1:4).

(2) Oh that he may kiss me with the kisses of his mouth
for your caresses are sweeter than wine!

(3) As to scent, your ointments are sweet,
Turaq oil is your name;
therefore maidens love you.

(4) Take me with you, let's run!
The king has brought me to his chambers.
We will be glad and rejoice in you;
we will extol your caresses more than wine;
rightly do they love you.

(5) Black am I, and comely,
O daughters of Jerusalem,
like tents of Kedar,
like curtains of Solomon.

Gerard Manley Hopkins borrows musical terminology to define both poetic works with smooth changes between their various parts and works with jarring, abrupt shifts.[12] The

---

[12] G. M. Hopkins, "On the Origins of Beauty," in *The Journals and Papers,* H.

former, with smooth transitions, he designates "chromatic."
The latter that employ devices that dwell on detail or on the
individual effect, he identifies as "diatonic." The diatonic scale
"leaves out" whereas the chromatic "puts in" the half tones.
We, in turn, recognize the centrifugal in Song of Songs in its
"diatonicity."

## Mosaic of Dazzling Images

Brilliant and overpowering individual images abound in the
Song, imparting a disjunctive tone. Among the exuberant types
of employment of imagery is the artistic juxtaposition of images
appealing to the various senses at one time. These intersensory
representations create a discontinuous reading, impeding the
flow of the poem. The artist does not merely appeal to the indi-
vidual senses distinctly and alternately, but conveys in the work
a synesthetic and undifferentiated sensitivity. Synesthesia is a
sensation in one part of the body produced by a stimulus applied
to another part. The poet replaces the conventional division
into five senses, and the analysis of experience into discrete
sense data, by employing intersensory imagery. The poet of the
Song describes visual or olfactory or other sense stimuli in terms
of effects transferred from their proper sphere.

The following passage exhibits striking sense-transfers which
give an idea of the range, novelty and power of the intersense
imagery in the Song of Songs. It also sets up the reader for simi-
lar examples later in the work.

> a  Draw me after you, let us run!
> b  The King brought me to his chambers.
> c  We will exult and rejoice in you,
> d  We will savor/extol your love above wine.
> e  . . . . (1:4)

After the dynamic and kinesthetic effect of the first two cola
(4 ab), the beloved announces the objective of the movement to
the King's chamber: "We will exult and rejoice in you" (4c). In
4d, the woman spells out the specific sensual modes of amorous
exultation and joy. The interplay of senses is apparent in the
verb, its object and the comparative, all three Hebrew words in
4d.

The verb *nazkīrāh* is not to be understood only as "let us
praise" (*NEB*) in accord with the usual meaning of the *hif'îl*

House, ed. (New York and Toronto: Oxford University Pres, 1959) 104; also cited in
Stankiewicz, "Centripetal," 222.

form of the root *zkr*, "mention," "extol," or "recite." Similarly, the verb is not to be construed exclusively "we shall inhale" as Robert Gordis does, according to the osmatic apprehension of burnt offerings as in Lev 24:7; Isa 66:3; Hos 14:8 and Ps 20:4.[13] AB and *NJPS* render it more felicitously as "savor" which unites the olfactory and gustatory senses. This is all the more appropriate in light of the conventional enjoyment of the taste *and* smell of fine wine with which love is compared in 4d. The poetic genius, throughout the Song, employs words of multiple significance arousing several senses. None of the denotations or connotations are to be ignored; good poetry provides several levels of meaning. "Praising," "smelling and "tasting" are each appropriate and to be understood in this colon.

The object of the verb is similarly evocative of several senses. *dōdīm*, "love(s)," "lovemaking" or "caresses" is certainly experienced with tactile sensors. However, the erotic and the intimate involve not only the tactile and/or cutaneous enjoyment of *dōdīm*, but also its gustatory and olfactory enjoyment (whether or not we construe the word as "breasts" which has the same ancient consonantal spelling as "loves," i.e., *ddm*). Support for this "tasting" and "smelling" of love and lovemaking is clear in the repeated comparison of love to "wine" throughout the song.

The third Hebrew word of 4d, *yayin*, "wine," exhibits a further extension of the multiple-sense imagery. The likening of love to wine recurs here and echoes the metaphor in 1:1. The power of the Song resides in the artist's choice of words that inspire a plethora of sensual associations. "Wine" is a parade example of such a word. On the one level wine provides gustatory enjoyment. On another level, the lover also appreciates the bouquet of fine wine. And on yet another level wine has a powerful effect on all the senses. It transports the individual, leading to full and complete sensual pleasures. Its association with the enjoyment of sex is patent throughout the Song as it also is in Gen 19:32. Wine's power to revive the sluggish is expressed in Prov. 31:6; its gladdening capability is indicated in Ps 104:15 and Eccl 10:19. Its connection with hospitality is seen in Prov. 9:3. The poet compares wine with love and the effects of love. Wine is expressive of well-being, happiness and youthful ardor. In the Song, wine and even the effects it produces lack any tinge of the unfavorable. On the

[13] R. Gordis, *The Song of Songs and Lamentations: A Study, Modern Translation and Commentary* [1954], rev. and aug. ed. (New York: KTAV, 1974).

contrary, these natural effects express the strong emotions that the couple experiences in the transports of their love. All wine's pleasurable qualities, however, pale in comparison with the delights of the lovers. The poet reiterates that love and lovemaking are *more* pleasurable than wine (1:2, 4; 4:10).

The Song is dealing with an abstraction, an emotion. The artist nonetheless succeeds in vividly conveying this feeling. Sense titillation serves to express the inexpressibility of love. The adventure of the young couple within the pastoral setting evokes the emotion of love in the Song of Songs. The correspondence between sensations, and the synesthetic imagery employed to convey the reality of that adventure startle the reader and catch attention as a new and curious form of expression. Thus primed, the reader appreciates the sensual and intersensory imagery throughout Canticles. A certain cohesion develops from the frequent occurrence of this remarkable figure.

At the same time that the centripetal effect is imparted, the daring and innovative figures exert a countervailing centrifugal force. These intersensory representations at each recurrence create a discontinuous reading that impedes the flow of the poem. A disjunctive pull is thus in tension with a unifying tug.

The reader is conditioned to identify, even expect, these multiply suggestive analogies. The representations of the lovers is a fine example. She is likened to a "lily among thorns" and he to an "apple (tree) among the trees of the forest" (2:2-3). The lily imagery suggests the fragrance, the appearance and the texture of the lily (and therefore, of the woman) in contrast to those of the thorn. Hence, the one simile evokes olfactory, visual and tactile sensations. The image also carries sensually erotic overtones gained from the association of lilies with the maiden's physical charms elsewhere in the Song (7:3, 4:5, 6:2, and 6:3). The single analogy of the apple in 2:3 suggests beauty, shade, flavor and fragrance, thereby appealing to the visual, tactile or cutaneous, gustatory and olfactory senses respectively. The recurrence of the apple imagery in the Song similarly arouses sexual associations (7:9, 8:3). The etymology of the word *tappūaḥ*, "apple," deriving from *npḥ* meaning to "breathe," "pant," or "blow," also indicates a connection with wafting breezes and/or aromas.

The mention of "apple" and "lily" stimulates sensual impressions and sexual association. When "apple" and "lily" are used as similes (2:2-3), they suggest multiple similarities drawn from different sensory domains. The effect of the manifold facets of such imagery is to stay the progress of the poem. The reader is led to dwell on the individual figure of speech, exploring its several levels. The continuity of the poem is thus broken and the centrifugal tendency is noted. The frequency of this phenomenon, however, imparts a characteristic tone to the work which ties it together. The two contrary forces create a dramatic tension.

Not only the individual image but the grouping of images contributes to the atomistic diffuseness of Song of Songs. A preference for rapidly shifting words, phrases and analogies is recognized in the Song. These sequences often present unexpected, even paradoxical combinations. Chapter 7:1-5 likens the maiden's body first to jewels, then to wine goblets, heaps of wheat, twin fawns, an ivory tower, water pools and a mountain tower in a dizzying line of similes. The body parts are depicted through extravagant and disparate likenesses.

The poet endeavors to create in hearers an emotion similar to the poet's own by presenting a series of lyrical images, likening the beloved's beauty to diverse common delights drawn from experience. The unrelated analogues are not representational. They do not combine to produce an integral mental picture. Rather than a tight integrality, the result is an aggregate with no fixed formal center.

The dazzling images do have a centripetal effect, nevertheless. On the thematic level, they convey the central and centralizing subject of the Song. This imagery is appropriate for the love experiences in the spring garden, not only because it has charm and the glamor of novelty and surprise, and not only because it gives embodiment to the abstract, but also because it enables the poet to describe the object from more than one angle. Two and more sensations coexist in the perception of the poet. Instead of separating them into distinct images in the artistic creation, the artist blends them into one composite impression conveying the fundamental unity and the atmosphere of the scene.

There is an additional factor contributing to the appositeness of the extravagant figures to the theme of the Song. The artist's experience of love transcends ordinary experience. Physical verisimilitude would not convey the height and depth of the emotion. The poetic defiance of common sense is the attempt to stretch conventional language, to rise above and go beyond the limits of ordinary language in order to transmit the exuberance of the artist's experience. Indeed, this is what Henry W. Wells designates the "exuberant image." "Two powerfully imaginative terms influence one another strongly while their relation remains vague and indefinite. A common loveliness for example may alone associate the ideas. . . . The more rational distinctions of sophisticated art are often cast aside. . . ."[14]

The crowding together in the Song of the great number of sense impressions reaches toward a state of intense sensitivity, conveying impressionistically the utmost height of the sensuous experience of the lovers.

> 4:10 a How beautiful are your caresses, my sister, my bride!
>      b How much sweeter your caresses than wine
>      c Your ointments more than any spice!
>   11 a Sweetness drops from your lips O bride;
>      b Honey and milk are under your tongue;
>      c And the scent of your robes is like the scent of Lebanon.

Almost each line arouses another sense sphere. Perhaps even hearing is alluded to in 4:11 a and b in which lips and tongue, the vehicles of speech, are mentioned. The unusual interactions and transferences of agreeable sensations experienced by the lovers in the spring outdoors suggest an irreducible profusion of entangled agreeable sensations that constitutes love itself. The language of logic is not the language of poetry. The craft of the poet is not merely an enumeration of the real and the objective, but the expression of that which results from the meeting of the poet and the reality. Thus, the peculiar heaping of sensual splendors in one passage does not present the verisimilar, but by means of the entire group, the poet suggests the superlative. No single sensual detail would be adequate. The alternating consecutive appeal to excellences in beauty, taste, fragrance, apparent in 4:10-11, implies the quintessence of emotion experienced by the couple. The manifold represents the singular.

## Ambiguity

A corollary of the profusion of uncommon words and forms in the Song is the high incidence of ambivalence of the individual word and polysemy in the text. I shall not argue my position in the controversy of intentional vs. fortuitous effects of poetry. As Kenneth Burke states in his discussion of the principles underlying the appeal of literature, I, too, maintain that ". . . a dis-

[14] H. W. Wells, *Poetic Imagery* (New York: Russel and Russel, 1961) 34.

cussion of effectiveness [in arousing emotions] in literature should be able too include unintended effects as well as intended ones."[15]

Among the numerous examples of literary ambiguity and multiple meaning in Song of Songs is 2:16c. The two Hebrew words rendered "who feeds on the lilies" can be construed in several ways. Marvin Pope, in his characteristically thorough manner, presents the many proposals.

> The crux of the issue is whether the participle of r'y, "pasture," "feed," is here used in the sense of eat, or cause to eat, and whether the flowers in question, the šôšannîm, indicate what is eaten or the locale of the feeding; whether the lover feeds on the flowers, or (on something else) among the flowers, or pastures (his flock) among the flowers.[16]

If we now refer to our explication (above of the analogy of the maiden to a lily in 2:2 and the subsequent erotic associations of the lily in the Song, we are struck by the poignant double entendre of "who feeds on the lilies." The multiplicity of significations highlights the centrifugal tendency in Song of Songs.

Poetic ambiguity is similarly seen in the depiction of Solomon's litter in 3:9-10:

> A litter King Solomon made for himself,
>     from the wood of Lebanon.
> Its posts he made of silver,
> its headrest of gold;
> it seat of purple [stuff]
> and its interior inlaid with 'ahăbāh.

G.R. Driver proposed that 'hb, the root of the 'ahăbāh, often translated "love" may also mean leather, after an Arabic cognate.[17] Support for this understanding comes from another Mediterranean source. Homer, puts in the mouth of Odysseus a description of the conjugal bed that Odysseus crafted for himself and Penelope.[18] The salient features of the Greek couch are remarkably analogous to those of Solomon's. In both, the bedposts are made of wood, gold and silver are the primary decorations, and purple is the prominent color. The inlay of

[15] K. Burke, *Counter-Statement* (Berkeley: University of California Press, 1968) 123.
[16] M. Pope, *Song of Songs*, AB 7C (Garden City, N.Y.: Doubleday, 1977) 405.
[17] G. R. Driver, "Supposed Arabisms in the Old Testament," *JBL* 55 (1936) 111.
[18] *The Odyssey* Book 33, lines 198-202.

Solomon's litter, *'ahăbāh*, understood in the sense of the Arabic, "leather," is precisely the material which completes Odysseus' couch, i.e., "thongs of oxhide."

The recognition of the biblical literary device of building up to a climactic variation also backs the multiple meaning. In Cant 3:10 the three initial cola establish a pattern, i.e., the mention of the part of the love couch plus its concrete substance. Taken in its usual meaning, the fourth and final member of the verse mentions the love couch part plus a significant deviation—an abstract noun instead of the concrete substance. This variation of the final parallel colon from the pattern established confounds the reader's expectation and maintains interest. The additional device of poetic ambiguity is also operative here.

The interior of the litter is indeed inlaid with both "love" and "leather." To reduce the poetry of the Song to the "one correct meaning" is to rob it of its distinctive appeal. That distinctive appeal, won in part by the use of double entendre, is on the centrifugal extreme of the continuum. The multiple meaning produces a momentary wavering on the part of the reader, who weighs which one or ones of the possible significations are appropriate. This impedes rather than accelerates the reading, by highlighting the part at the expense of the whole.

The effect of the poetic ambiguity is not exclusively centrifugal. At the moment the reader understands that two or more interpretations are appropriate in the particular text, the vacillation ends and a greater integration ensues. The multiple meaning brings together various aspects or levels of the work. One meaning coheres with one facet while another meaning picks up another facet. Thus, two loose ends are gathered by one polysemous word, phrase or structure.

A commonly used device in the Song is the metaphor that highlights an ambiguous antecedent. This locution typically mentions A, likens A to B and then provides a predication that is equally appropriate for A and B. A few examples will clarify this trope or figure of speech.

> 1:13  A bundle of myrrh is my beloved to me;
>        Between my breasts *he/it* spends the night.

In Hebrew, the preformative *y-* on "spends the night" designates the third person, masculine, singular subject pronoun. "He" or "it" is equally fitting. The bundle of myrrh and the beloved both find rest in the woman's bosom.

> 2:3 Like an apple tree among the trees of the forest,
> So is my beloved among the lads.
> In *his/its* shadow I long to sit
> And *his/its* fruit is sweet to my palate.

The Hebrew suffix -*ō* affixed to "shadow" and "fruit" is the possessive pronoun rendered either "his" or "its." In 2:3 the woman seeks the shadow of her beloved as well as the shadow of the apple tree; she longs for the fruit of his love (cf. 4:13-16; 5:16) just as she desires the apple of the tree.

> 2:9 My beloved resembles a deer or a young gazelle.
> Behold *he/it* (*zeh*) stands behind our wall
> Looking through our window,
> Peering through the lattice!

Who is outside the house? A deer or a dear one? *Zeh* translated "he/it" is the object of the exclamation "behold" (cf. 2:8) and is suitable for either of the two masculine singular antecedents.

> 5:13 his lips are lilies
> *dripping* flowing myrrh

The feminine plural participial form of *nṭp*, "drip," can refer here to the beloved's lips (cf. 4:11) or to the perfumed lilies or indeed to the beloved's lips *and* to the perfumed lilies.

## Architectonics

The attempts at a "logical" analysis of the work as a literary whole are generally unable to demonstrate convincingly that there is indeed movement to a conclusion in the work. "Matters are as far advanced in 1:4 or 2:4 as they are in 8:4."[19]

J. Angénieux, in contrast to his predecessors, based his division of parts more on structural form than on the presumed sense of the work.[20] His identification of initial and final refrains, spatial and temporal circumstances, opening and closing themes, distinctive themes and secondary refrains, resulted in a

[19] Meek, *IB* 5, 92.
[20] J. Angénieux, "Structure du Cantique des Cantiques," *ETL* 41 (1965) 96-142; "Les trois portraits du Cantique des Cantiques," *ETL* 42 (1966) 582-96; and "Le Cantique des Cantiques en huit chants et refrains alternants," *ETL* 44 (1968) 87-140.

"reconstituted" text that considerably distorted the received text.[21] Thus, in the name of literary dramatic unity, Angénieux "created" an integral whole.

J. C. Exum followed Angénieux's form method for arriving at her division of the poetic text of the Song.[22] On the basis of repetitions of words, phrases and motifs, Exum isolated poetic units, examined them and fixed parallels among them. Her work, marked by a respect for the received text, presents an inclusio patterning as the major structure of the Song. Cant. 1:2-26 and 8:4-14 constitute the two poems that frame four others. Exum's analysis, however, teeters between discovery and contrivance. Some of the key words she identifies are too common and too randomly collocated to serve as structural markers. Her basis for demarcation and isolation of poems, therefore, often appears too scanty and tenuous. Great value attaches, nevertheless, to Exum's work. Her excellent literary sense uncovers effective use of stylistic devices and a high artistry in the Song.

Another contemporary researcher studying the structure of the Song is William Shea. Shea sees a grand chiastic patterning as the guiding principle of the ancient poet's organization of Canticles.[23] Shea points to common themes, pictures and dreams in the following segments:

```
A  1:2  - 2:2
   B  2:3  - 2:17
      C  3:1  - 4:16
      C' 5:1  - 7:10
   B' 7:11 - 8:5
A' 8:6 - 8:14
```

The correspondence of the segments serves to link the first series of three (A, B, C) with their inversion in the second series (C', B', A'). Shea's work is marred by an arbitrariness and ann attempt to force the units to fit his schema. Francis Landy effectively criticizes Shea's excesses and errors: "The smallest correspondence in the right place is enough to produce a chiasmus (e.g. the word *kesep* "silver" in 1:11 and 8:11); while inconvenient echoes are totally ignored (e.g. 3:4, 8:2)."[24]

The peculiar structure of the Song of Songs does not accept

21 Angénieux, "Les trois portraits."
22 J. C. Exum, "A Literary and Structural Analysis of the Song of Songs," *ZAW* 85 (1973) 47-79.
23 W. Shea, "The Chiastic Structure of the Song of Songs," *ZAW* 92 (1980) 378-96.
24 F. S. Landy, *Paradoxes of Paradise: Identity and Difference in the Song of Songs* (Sheffield: The Almond Press, 1983) 40; cf. 296, nn. 99, 100, 101.

the imposition of tight, regular patterns. The composition of Canticles is essentially open and loose. The aesthetic effect of the Song is heightened by the tension between its prevailing centrifugal structure and partially countervailing centripetal forces.

## Repetitions and Associations

The centripetal forces active in the work are not of the usual kind. There is no clear logical development nor is there a regular division into symmetrically ordered parts. Although Exum and Shea do not propose sufficiently compelling and convincing schematic designs in Canticles, their identifications of parallels, cross-references, and recurring motifs in the Song are significant. These interconnections among the parts of the text provide the crucial structural balance in the work. Without these centripetal forces in the composition of the Song, disintegration would result. Small constituent elements would break apart; unity and wholeness would be lost. Indeed, the fragmentary features distinguish the work. I therefore locate the Song's predominant structural character near the centrifugal extreme of the continuum. The dynamism of Canticles derives from the tension and balance of the parts with each other and with the totality. This equipoise is the result of countervailing forces. Centripetality does not prevail but its force, too, is apparent.

The recurrence of identical or slightly varied phrases abounds in the Song. The restatements do not occur at regular intervals as do refrains, and are therefore not as effective in demarcating a poem's formal structure. This accounts in no small measure for the varied and unsuccessful determinations of the boundaries of the Song's segments. The positive consequences of the study of repetends is that they feature the intricate interconnectedness of the work. "Repetends" are defined as "phrases, verses, or short passages that recur sometimes in different forms, at varying intervals."[25]

In order to show to what a great degree the interlacings of repetends and other associations knit the work into a centripetal web I shall examine, by way of example, no more than a few of the correspondences that echo and recall the first verse of the Song (1:2) following the superscription. I shall also try to ac-

---

[25] M. V. Fox, *The Song of Songs and the Ancient Egyptian Love Songs* (Madison: University of Wisconsin Press, 1985) 210. Fox introduces this useful term into the study of Song of Songs, quoting its definition from the *Princeton Encyclopedia of Literature* (1974) 699.

count for the basis of the associations. I emphasize that the following pages analyze only one verse and some of its ramifications. To understand the intricacy of the texture and the density of the weave one should bear in mind that each verse in the Song casts similar projections and sends out analogous rays that touch all parts of the work. The Song teems with phonological, lexical, syntactic and imagistic associations—inextricably bound with no logical order.

> 1:2 *yiššāqēnī minnĕšīqōt pīhū kī ṭōbīm dōdeykā*
>      *miyyāyin*
> May he kiss me with the kisses of his mouth for
> sweeter are your caresses than wine.
>
> 8:1 . . . *'eššāqĕkā gam lō' yābūzū lī*
> I will kiss you and none will despise me.
>
> 8:2 . . . *'ašqĕkā miyayin hāreqaḥ mē'ăsīs rimmōnī*
> I will give you to drink spiced wine and juice of my
> pomegranate.

On the phonological level, the *š*, *q*, and *k* sounds reverberate. Even though the words derive from different stems (1:2 *nšq*, "kiss"; 8:1 *nšq*, "kiss"; but 8:2 *šqh*, "give drink"), the like sounds echo in one another (cf. Gen 29:10-11).

Direct repetition associates 1:2 and 8:2; *yayin* "wine" appears in both verses.

A further correspondence between 1:2 and 8:1 is on the thematic level. In the former, he will kiss her and in the latter she will kiss him. This inversion suggests a reciprocity and mutuality in their love. Stylistically, the inversion exemplifies the principle of repetition with variation that is so common in the Bible.

> 1:4 *nazkīrāh dōdeykā miyyayin*
> we will savor/extol your caresses more than wine

The co-occurrence of *yayin*, "wine," and *dōdīm*, "caresses," in 1:2 and 1:4 binds the two together.

> 4:10 . . . *māh ṭōbū dōdayik miyyayin wĕrēaḥ*
>       *šĕmānayik mikkōl bĕšāmīm*
> Oh how much sweeter are your caresses than wine
> and the scent of your ointments more than all the
> spices.

The linking of 1:2 and 4:10 is tighter than the mere repetition of the analogy of caresses and wine. We have here a particular "associative sequence" common to both verses. Fox

describes this concept as "groups of words, sentences, or motifs
... that recur in the same order even though that order does not
seem required by narrative sequence or logical continuity."[26]
The end of 1:2 exhibits three Hebrew stems that recur in pre-
cisely the same order in 4:10: *ṭōb, dōdīm,* and *yayin* ("sweet,"
"caresses" and "wine"). The associative sequence, however,
does not end here. After likening caresses to the sweetness of
wine, the poet introduces another comparison involving the fra-
grance of oils or ointments. This analogy begins with the word
*rēaḥ,* "scent" and proceeds directly to *šĕmāneykā,* "your (masc.)
ointments" in 1:2 and *šĕmānayik,* "your (fem.) ointments" in
4:10. Thus, the recurrence of five elements, *ṭōb, dōdīm,
miyyyim, rēaḥ,* and *šĕmānīm,* in the identical order creates a
strong affinity between 1:2 and 4:10.

> 4:3 ... *kĕḥūṭ haššānī śiptōtayik ūmidbārēk nā'weh* ...
> ... like a scarlet thread are your lips and your mouth
> is comely ...

Another thread drawn through the text of the Song appears
on the lexico-semantic level or that of word meaning. Literary
cohesion is achieved through the association of lexical items that
regularly co-occur. Not only direct repetition, but the colloca-
tion of synonyms and near synonyms binds various parts. Note
the near synonymy of *peh,* "mouth" (*pīhū,* "his mouth," in 1:2)
with *midbar,* "organ of speech (= mouth) (*midbārēk,* "your
mouth," in 4:3).

> 2:3 *ūpiryō mātōq lĕhikkī*
> and his [or "its"] fruit is sweet to my palate

*ṭobim,* "sweet," conjures up verses in which that word figures.
The word also calls to mind the near synonym *mātōq,* "sweet":

> 5:16 *ḥikkō mamtaqīm wĕkullō maḥmadīm*
> his palate is sweet drink (cf. Neh 8:10); he is all a
> delight

The multiple associations of 1:2, 4:3 and 5:16 include the sy-
nonymy of *ṭōb* and *mātōq,* "sweet" and also the correspondence
of *pīhū,* "his mouth," *midbārēk,* "your mouth," and *ḥikkō,* "his
palate."

[26] Fox, *The Song,* 215.

7:10 *wĕḥikkēk kĕyēyn ḥaṭṭōb*
and your palate is like sweet wine

Here, too, as in 5:16 the word *ḥēk*, "palate," appears. "Palate" and "mouth" are drawn from the same lexical set. "Palate" stands in the recognizable semantic relation of synecdoche to mouth, of part for the whole. They evoke one another and other members of the same more general class of oral and adjacent facial features.

The density of the web is extraordinary. The "mouth" resonates in the text at each mention of "lips," "tongue," "teeth," "cheeks" and "palate." The terms for the mouth, the parts thereof, and the facial features, are numerous in Canticles. They all tie in with 1:2.

> 1:4 *hĕbi'anī 'el bēyt hayyayin wĕdiglō 'ălay 'ahăbāh*
> he brought me to the house of wine and his
> banner over me is love

*yayin*, "wine" is a most expressive term in Song of Songs. The explicit co-occurrence of "wine" and "caresses" and "love" (1:2, 1:4, 2:4, 4:10, 5:1, 8:2) leads to the identity of the terms. There is, in fact, no mention of wine in the Song that is not closely tied to love. The poet uses "wine" metaphorically in 5:1. The analogy of wine/love is explained in the final colon of 5:1: "eat, O friends, drink to intoxification of love." Prov 7:18 uses a similar locution. The prostitute accosts the unsuspecting lad and proffers a night of lovemaking with the words *nirweh dōdīm*, "let's drink deeply of love." The "house of wine" = "house of love." The "kiss," understood in *'ašqĕkā*, "I will give you drink [spiced wine]," equates the two as does each allusion to wine and lovemaking.

> 1:3 *lĕrēaḥ šĕmāneykā ṭōbīm šemen tūraq šĕmekā 'al-kēn*
> *'ălāmōt 'ăhēbūkā*
> As to scent, your ointments are sweet./ Turaq oil is
> your name / Therefore the maidens love you.

Also on the phonological level, the repetition of the *š* sound extends and links 1:2 with 1:3, which continues the play on that sound. The superscription, too, evidences the same play and may have been chosen to foreground the assonance of the following two verses all the more.

The multiple recurrence of the same sound in close proxim-

ity at the very outset of the work predisposes the
reader/listener to other aural plays.

> 7:14 *haddūdā'īm nātĕnū rēaḥ*
> The mandrakes give forth fragrance

The word *dōdeykā*, "your caresses," in 1:2 reverberates
throughout the work. The word is ambiguous which adds to its
associative power. In the Song, *dōd* denotes "beloved" in the
singular or plural. The plural may also denote "caresses."
There are a full 36 occurrences of this word in its various forms
in one or another of these two meanings in Canticles. Certainly
36 appearances of a word in a total text of only 117 verses lend a
centripetal tendency and cohesiveness to the work. In 7:14
there is, in addition, *dūdā'īm*, "mandrakes," a word related to
*dōd* both phonologically and semantically. This suggestive word
is collocated with *nātĕnū rēaḥ*, "give forth fragrance," and fol-
lows immediately upon "there will I give my caresses to you."
*dūdā'īm* were understood in the ancient world as exciting sexual
desire (cf. Gen 30:14, 15 *bis*, 16). Thus, the sensual, erotic, pho-
nological and thematic ties between 1:2 and 7:14 contribute to
the compactness of Song of Songs.

While progressing through Song of Songs, the reader con-
stantly recalls the multiply evocative verses already read. Our
examination of the associations and repetitions of 1:2 through-
out the Song highlights their centripetal power. In the face of
fragmenting figures, the recurrence of words, themes, sounds,
and images constantly brings the parts back to an equilibrium
with the whole.

### Parallel Pieces—The waṣfs

The recurrence in the Song of scenes, episodes, and themes
is also a strong unifying force. Among these are the descriptions
of the physical beauty of the woman and her beloved, the adju-
ration and the nocturnal search for the beloved. Murphy per-
ceptively noted, "What needs to be recognized here is the
evidence of the dramatic presentation of love-experiences that
continually repeat themselves."[27]
The descriptions and praises of the physical charms of the
lovers command a prominent position in the Song. The *waṣf*, as
this type of song of praise is commonly designated, recurs in 4:1-
7, 5:10-16 and 7:27. In a briefer form, 6:5-7 duplicates some

---

[27] Murphy, "The Unity," 443.

lines from 4:1-7. Typically the *wasf* isolates individual body parts and provides an elaborate metaphor for each. The rapidly shifting, kaleidoscopic centrifugal imagery is taken from disparate realms with no common thread. The discontinuity of the figures is manifest in 7:1-7.[28] The aesthetic greatness of Canticles lies in part in its manipulation of advancing and arresting features. To be sure, the individual likenesses in 7:1-7 proceed from the diverse domains of man-made products, natural phenomena, farming, and animals. But the discrete metaphors are kept at short tether by the strict directionality of the body-part referents. Although the "vehicle" ranges over wide territory, the "tenor" is anchored in a cohesive graphic order. The maiden's body is represented from foot to head in 7:1-7. Further, a framing figure lends a homogeneity to this segment. "Oh how beautiful are your steps. . ." (7:2) is answered by "Oh how beautiful and delightful you are" (7:7).

In 5:10-16 she celebrates the beauty of the lad's body—a counterpart to his extolling of her physical beauty. This inversion of praiser and praised is complemented by another inversion. In 5:10-16 she celebrates his beautiful body parts from head to foot. This *wasf*, too, is enclosed by an inclusio figure. The daughters of Jerusalem pose the question: "How is your beloved better than others?" in 5:9. In 5:16, her answer ends in the words, "this is my beloved, O daughters of Jerusalem."

Another description of the woman's body appears at 4:1-7. In these verses, different parts of the maiden's anatomy seriatim are each complemented by a simile. Note that in the seven verses there are six cases of the *kaf* of similitude! Although a clear head-to-foot or foot-to-head directionality is not apparent, the repeated *kaf* exerts a unifying force on the series. There is also an inclusio here, marking off the *wasf*: "Behold you are beautiful, my love, behold you are beautiful" in 4:1 is echoed in 4:7, "You are altogether beautiful, my love."

The description in 7:1-7 strongly echoes the 4:1-7 description. In particular, 4:5 and 7:4 concur in their representation of the breasts; 4:4 and 7:5 agree on the portrayal of the neck; 4:1 and 7:5 conform on the depiction of the eyes. The description of the eyes and the lips of the man, too, recall those of the woman (cf. 5:12 and 7:5; 5:13 and 4:11). The various parts of the work are continually interlocked by such restatements of words, phrases, and larger units such as the *wasf*. Murphy accounts for

---

[28] This is against Alter's view: ". . .a lovely illustration of how the exuberant metaphors carry the action forward (*The Art of Biblical Poetry* [New York: Basic Books, 1985] 198).

these repetitions: "The man and woman never tire of saying the same things to each other: how beautiful the other is, personal longing. . . ."[29]

## Parallel Pieces—The Adjurations

In the span of the eight chapters of Song of Songs there figure prominently several word clusters that create a distinct poetic texture to the entire book. The oath concerning the inciting of love is such a recurring piece. The adjuration appears at 2:7 and 3:5 in the identical form and again at 8:4 with slight variations. A suggestive fourth adjuration also appears (5:8) and calls to mind the other three. The recurrence of the same and similar segments arouses a feeling of familiarity and recognition and encourages reminiscence and recollection. In the case of the adjuration theme, the oaths themselves, and the immediate context of the three are similar. Each occurrence is directly preceded by a passage telling of the holding and embracing of the man and woman: 2:6 and 8:3 state the identical "his left hand under my head and his right hand embraces me"; 3:4 has "I held him and will not let him go until I bring him to my mother's house." The mention of bringing the beloved to the mother's house has its echo in 8:2, "I will lead you, I will bring you to my mother's house. . ." A further paralleling in the reappearances of this theme is the nighttime episode of search in the city for the beloved. Two occurrences of this motif figure in both instances in apposition before the oath theme: 3:1-5 and 5:5-7. This repetend and its accompanying elements recur in the same textual order in several places throughout the book. Although not at fixed intervals, their mutual association contributes to the close knit of Canticles. The earlier occurrences resonate in each subsequent occasion.

Fox presents and co-occurrences of this repetend and other shorter restated phrases and sentences in a clear format of side-by-side columns.[30] The degree of similarity and difference in these repetitions is readily apparent as are the major threads creating the texture of the work. These threads include the following "refrains" not adduced earlier:

---

[29] Murphy, "The Unity," 442.
[30] Fox, The Song, 211-14, 216.

seeing the blossoms of the vines and pomegranates
  (2:12, 13; 6:11; 7:13, 14)
expression of mutual belonging (2:15; 6:3; 7:11)
grazing among the lilies (2:16; 4:5 6:3)
lovesickness (2:5; 5:8)

## Parallelism Formulae

The repetitions are not only situated to create distant echoing. Reiteration plays a part within individual verses and over the brief span of a few consecutive verses. There is a recognized tendency in Canticles to employ a particular rhetorical device that plays on repetition within the structure of a single or of a few verses. Although this poetic device is only sporadic in Canticles, its appearance in one part suggests the other parts evidencing the same form of verse design. A degree of cohesion results which functions in part to balance the Song's strong centrifugality. Edward L. Greenstein[31] and Chayim Cohen[32] employ the term "staircase parallelism" to this type of repetition.[33]

> A sentence is started, only to be interrupted by an epithet or vocative. The sentence is then resumed from the beginning again, without the intervening epithet, to be completed in the second or third line.[34]The first appearance of staircase parallelism in Canticles is at 1:15:

> > Behold, you are beautiful, my love,
> > Behold you are beautiful;
> > Your eyes are doves.

The repetitive mechanism extends beyond the simple staircase parallelism. After the repeated element in 1:15 *hinnāk yāpāh*, "behold, you are beautiful," 1:16 opens with the same expression, with the gender changed: *hinnĕkā yāpeh dōdî*, "behold, you are beautiful [= handsome] my love." The concatenation of poetic cola is drawn out to the end of 1:16. The second colon of 1:16 begins *'ap nā'îm*, "indeed delightful."

---

[31] E. L. Greenstein, "Two Variations of Grammatical Parallelism in Canaanite Poetry and Their Psycholinguistic Background," *JANES* 6 (1974) 87-105.

[32] C. Cohen, "Studies in Early Israelite Poetry I: An Unrecognized Case of Three-Line Staircase Parallelism in the Song of the Sea," *JANES* 7 (1975) 13-17.

[33] Other designations for this phenomenon include "climactic parallelism," "repetitive parallelism," "expanded colon," and "incremental repetition."

[34] W. G. E. Watson, *Classical Hebrew Poetry: A Guide to Its Techniques* JSOTSup (Sheffield: *JSOT* Press, 1984) 150.

The first word is an affirmative particle. The same affirmative particle *'ap*, "indeed" begins the final colon of 1:16.

Chap. 4 is a showcase for repetition and wordplay in the Song. Staircase parallelism figures in the greatest concentration in this chapter.

> 4:1  *hinnāk yāpāh ra 'yātī*
> *hinnāk yāpāh 'ēynayik yōnīm*
> Behold you are beautiful, my
> love
> Behold you are beautiful;
> Your eyes are doves

The same medium and the same message as 1:15.

> 4:8a  *'ittī millĕbānōn kallāh*
> b  *'ittī millĕbānōn tābō 'ī*
> c  *tāšūrī mērō 'š 'ămānāh*
> d  *mērō 'š šnīr wĕhermōn*
> e  *mimĕ 'ōnōt 'ărāyōt*
> f  *mēharĕrēy nĕmērīm*
> With me from Lebanon, my bride,
> With me from Lebanon, come;
> Travel from atop Amana,
> From atop Senir and Hermon,
> From dens of lions,
> From mountains of leopards.

This six-line verse begins with staircase parallelism, repeating *'ittī millĕbānōn*, "with me from Lebanon," in a and b. A second repeated element, *mērō 'š*, "from atop," appears in c and d. Fox suggests that the place names and animal names in this verse "were chosen to call to mind the names of spices and sweet things."[35] Thus, he explains *lĕbānōn—lĕbōnāh* ("frankincense"), *'ărāyōt* ("lions")—*'ārītī* ("taste") and perhaps *nĕmērīm* ("leopards")—*mōr* ("myrrh") and *rō 'š* ("peak")—*rā 'šēy* (*bĕšāmīm*) ("best spices"). These allusions certainly tighten the work by the strong cross-referencing and complement the tightening of the verse by its word repetitions.

> 4:9  *libbabtinnī 'ăhōtī kallāh*
> *libbabtinnī bĕ 'ahad mē 'ēynayik*
> *bĕ 'ahad 'ănāq missawrōnayik*
> You have taken my heart, my sister, my bride;
> You have taken my heart, with one of your eyes,

---

[35] Fox, *The Song*, 135.

With one jewel of your necklace.

Notice the repeated element *libbabtinnī*, "you have taken my heart," in the staircase parallelism. The linking of elements in this verse hangs on the sounds ʾ, *ḥ*, *t* and *d* in *ʾăḥōtī*, *bĕʾaḥad (bis)* and the final elements *-nayik* in *mēʿēynayik* and *miṣṣawrōnayik*

> 4:10 *māh yāpū dōdayik ʾăḥōtī kallāh*
>      *māh ṭōbū dōdayik miyyayin*
>      *wĕrēaḥ šĕmānayik mikkōl bĕśāmīm*
>      How beautiful your caresses, my sister, my bride,
>      How [much] sweeter your caresses than wine
>      And the fragrance of your ointments than all spices.

The repeated element of the staircase parallelism here too is but one of the repetitions to note. The intervening element *ʾăḥōtī kallāh*, "my sister, my bride," is the same as in 4:9 above and 4:12 below. Furthermore, half of the element appeared in 4:8 *kallāh*, "bride."

> 4:12 *gan nāʿūl ʾăḥōtī kallāh*
>      *gal nāʿūl maʿyan ḥātūm*
>      A garden locked [is] my sister, my bride;
>      A fountain locked, a sealed spring.

I have gathered the examples of staircase parallelism in Chap. 4 and commented briefly on other aspects of repetition that appear prominently along with the staircase pattern. There is, in addition, a full array of interlocking puns and allusions that intertwine the parts of the chapter, summoning to mind other significant collocations of the suggestive words. *Ṭōbū dōdeykā miyyayin*, "sweeter are your caresses than wine," recalls 1:2 and the full constellation of verses with this repetend. The phrase also interlocks with "I drink my wine" and "eat and drink to intoxification of love" in 5:1. *bĕśāmīm* (4:10) recurs in 4:14, reverberates in 4:16 (*bĕśāmāyw*, "its/his spices") and in 5:1 (*bĕśāmī*, "my spice"). *dĕbaš wĕḥālāb*, "honey and milk" of 4:11 resounds in 5:1 also (*dibšī*, "my honey," and *ḥălābī*, "my milk"). *maʿyan gannīm*, "garden spring" in 4:15 resonates in 4:16 (*gannī*, "my garden" and *gannō*, "his garden"). *maʿyan ḥātūm*, "a fountain locked" in 4:12 is picked up in *maʿyan* of *maʿyan gannīm* in 4:15. *pĕrī mĕgādīm*, "luscious fruits" (4:13) comes to mind in 4:16, *pĕrī mĕgādāyw*, "his luscious fruits."

Chap. 6 opens with another example of staircase or incremental parallelism.

6:1 'ānāh hālak dōdēk hayyāpāh bannāšīm
    'ānāh pānāh dōdēk ūnĕbakkĕšennū 'immāk
    Where has your beloved gone, O beautiful one
        among the women?
    Where has your beloved turned, for we shall seek
        him with you?

There is a slight variation from the pure staircase parallelism
here. The repeated element includes a near synonym in place
of the original verb pānāh, "turned" for hālak, "went." The ef-
fect of holding the verse together and forcing a recapitulation
remains the same.

6:9 'aḥat hī⁻ yōnātī⁻ tammātī⁻
    'aḥat hī⁻ lĕ'immāh . . .
    She is unique, my dove, my perfect one
    She is unique to her mother.

Here we have the incremental parallelism and rhyme of the
final long -ī⁻sound in hī⁻ twice (this word appears a third time in
the continuation of the verse), yōnātī, and tammātī⁻.
    Chap. 7 also begins with this parallelism pattern:

7:1 šūbī⁻ šūbī⁻ haššūlammīt
    šūbī⁻ šūbī⁻ wĕneḥĕzeh bāk
    māh teḥĕzū baṣṣūlammīt
    kimĕḥōlat hammaḥănāyim
    Turn, turn O Shulamite,
    Turn, turn that we may view you.
    Why will you view the Shulamite
    in the dance of two camps?

Striking here, is the reduplication of virtually every word in the
verse. Particularly noteworthy is the fourfold repetition of the
first word šūbī⁻ and the dual ending on the final word
maḥănayim.

8:5 šāmāh ḥibbĕlātĕkā 'immekā
    šāmmāh ḥibbĕlāh yĕlādātĕkā
    There your mother conceived you
    There conceived she who bore you

In this case of staircase parallelism the repeated element in
the second line varies slightly. The second person feminine sin-
gular pronominal suffix was transferred from the verb, ḥibbĕlāh

to the noun *yĕlādātĕkā*.[36]

The employment of parallelism formulae and poetic devices is eclectic and irregular in the Song and therefore fragmentary and atomizing in respect to the totality of the book. The basis of many of the varied stylistic features, however, is repetition (of one type or another) which provides a tension with the loosening irregular formulae. Also, it is precisely the sporadic appearance, the faint echo, and the veiled allusion in Canticles that imparts a degree of cohesiveness to the text. The same elements that account for the work's centrifugal predominance alternately exert a centralizing, centripetal force which exerts a structural counterweight.

[36] D. Grossberg, "Noun/Verb Parallelism: Syntactic or Asyntactic," *JBL* 99 (1980) 488.

# CHAPTER 3

# LAMENTATIONS

The Songs of Ascents display an artistic tension between loosening and tightening forces within and among the fifteen discrete psalms and the whole of the Songs of Ascents. The Song of Songs exhibits a compositional structure marked by predominant, fragmenting features which tend toward a prevailing emphasis on the parts. This compositional design places Song of Songs near the centrifugal extreme on a centripetal/centrifugal continuum. Lamentations displays close, more conjunctive elements among its parts than do the Songs of Ascents or certainly Song of Songs. Lamentations is, thus, more centripetally oriented than the other two corpora. The twofold typology does not demand an absolute dichotomy. Each work shows tendencies of both centripetal and centrifugal types.

In this chapter, I identify and discuss complexes of features working within Lamentations. The concerted effect of these sometimes opposing features creates a dynamic tension and balance of the part with each other and with the whole. The simple setting of Lamentations at either extreme of the centrifugal/centripetal continuum does not reckon with the delicate balance of both tendencies that characterizes the book.

The prevailing theme, acrostic design, poetic meter, association of stanzas, perspectival shifts, verbal linking and echoing, historicity, imagery and closural devices are among the structural and thematic features which exert their respective loosening and tying forces. The complex of interrelated features makes the work hover between the centripetal and centrifugal extremes.

## Theme and Variations

The theme of the Book of Lamentations is the destruction of Jerusalem in 587 B.C.E. The book describes the suffering of the entire nation during and in the wake of this disaster. The poet's treatment of this single theme is at odds with the literary means employed. Each of the five chapters of the book constitutes a separate elegy on the fall of the nation. On one level, then, the book is an aggregate of five distinct poems sharing a single theme. Thus, Lamentations evidences a tension between an atomizing, centrifugal composition and a unifying centripetal structure—between the one theme and the five variations. Chaps. 1, 2, and 4 each begins with the common elegiac exclamation 'ēykāh ("Ah, how!").[1] This cry of grief reflects the central concern of the book. The same heading on three of the five poems also tends to tie and bind them into a whole.

### Acrostic Structure

The acrostic form is another consolidating element. To some degree all five poems partake of an alphabetic design. Both chaps. 1 and 2 have twenty-two stanzas of three lines each (1:7 and 2:19 are exceptions with four lines each). Each of the stanzas begins with a successive letter of the Hebrew alphabet in its proper order.[2] Chap. 3 is a more ambitious acrostic than the others. It is built on the triple employment of the alphabet. Instead of merely beginning each three-line stanza with a successive letter of the alphabet, the poet begins each of the three lines of each stanza with the appropriate letter. Chap. 4 is similar to chaps. 1 and 2 in that each stanza begins with another letter of the alphabet in its proper sequence. In chap. 4, however, there are two lines to each stanza and not three as in chaps. 1, 2, and 3. Although chap. 5 is not properly an acrostic, it has precisely twenty-two lines (as do Pss 33, 38, and 103). The twenty-two lines conform to the number of letters in the Hebrew alphabet. It may be assumed that this was deliberate on the part of the poet to suggest the alphabet.

The motivation for the alphabetic basis of structure may have been to provide a mnemonic tool. The acrostic thus facilitates recall and integrates the various lines and stanzas into one poetic work, albeit in an artificial manner. The motive for the acrostic design may also have been to display the poet's virtuosity, the ability to create within artistic restraints. Furthermore, the acrostic might have been employed to express "totality," "from A to Z." Regardless of the authorial intention, the alphabetic pattern brings together disparate lines, impresses them on the memory, shows the artist's ability and makes of the

---

[1] 'ykh or 'yk also appears as an exclamation of lamentation in 2 Sam 1:19; Isa 1:21; Jer 2:21; 9:19; 48:17; Mic 2:4; and Eccl 2:16.

[2] There is a minor variation in the order of the 'ayin and peh in the chapters of Lam. In chaps. 1 and 3 the 'ayin precedes the peh as it does in the Hebrew alphabet that has become normative today. In chaps. 2 and 4 these two letters appear in reverse order.

many parts one artistic whole. The acrostic expresses a full and complete set and not merely an arbitrary listing of units. The work balances on the line between unity and diversity, blending the many and varied expressions of grief into one unified elegy.

## qīnāh *Meter*

The careful arrangement of the chapters within Lamentations lends a pattern to what might otherwise emerge as a redundant aggregate. The patterning tightens the work. Crescendo and diminuendo mark this unity. The build-up of poetic form begins in chaps. 1 and 2 with the single alphabetic acrostic characterizing their twenty-two stanzas. Chap. 3 is the acrostic showcase of the book, the center of the text, and the ideological focus of the work. Here, a crescendo in form is reached with the threefold acrostic. A successive letter of the alphabet opens and adorns each of the three lines of each of the twenty-two stanzas. Following this tour de force, the poet modifies the alphabetic stratagem into a diminuendo of poetic power. Chap. 4 exhibits but a single alphabetic acrostic in a poem of only two-line stanzas. The decrescendo comes to its end in the twenty-two lines of chap. 5 where the mere suggestion of the alphabet is the ultimate in the gradual diminution of the acrostic device. The makeup of each stanza also furthers the decrescendo. A *triplet* of bicola constitutes each stanza of chaps. 1, 2, and 3. Each stanza of chap. 4 carries a *couplet* of bicola. Chap. 5 exhibits a *single* bicolon in each stanza.

William H. Shea grapples with the poetic question of the whole vs. the parts when he states that "acrostics were utilized in the composition of Lamentations for the express purpose of defining a precise structure of the work as a whole."[3] Shea proceeds to propose that the form for that structure is one of qīnāh or lament meter. This term emanates from K. Budde[4] who wrote the classical description of a distinctive meter he perceived in Lamentations. He found the poetic line broken into two parts, the first typically possessing three accentual units and the second, two. This peculiar "longer plus shorter" meter characterizes chaps. 1-4 of Lamentations and recurs in other parts of the Hebrew Bible written in an elegiac strain. Budde claimed that this is the rhythm peculiar to Hebrew elegy.[5] A further

---

[3] W. H. Shea, "The qīnāh Structure of the Book of Lamentations," *Bib* 60 (1979) 103.

[4] K. Budde, "Das hebraische Klaglied," *ZAW* 2 (1882) 1-52.

[5] W. R. Garr also studied the qīnāh and progressed significantly beyond Budde. Garr concluded that within the meter described by Budde, "the poet fashions his

trait of this poetry is the imperfect echoing and paralleling of
the longer first colon by the shorter second colon. S. R. Driver
wrote that the first colon "seems, as it were, to die away in it
[the second colon], and a plaintive, melancholy cadence is thus
produced."[6] This particular meter has therefore been called
qīnāh meter. Not all elegies show the qīnāh meter and some
poems clearly not elegies do evidence the meter. Song of Songs
is a case in point. The meter of Canticles is predominantly the
qīnāh; the theme, however, is obviously not elegiac. Modern
scholars, therefore, consider it a misnomer. In general, never-
theless, the description of the meter in Lamentations is valid.

Shea argues that the generally apparent three stress-accents
followed by two stress-accents in the poetic bicola of Lamenta-
tions is but one application of the qīnāh meter and that "on the
smallest scale." The overall structure of the five-chapter book of
Lamentations is an example of the qīnāh pattern "on the
grandest scale." Shea points first to the first three longer chap-
ters which display triplets of bicola comprising each alphabetic
unit. He then notes the final two shorter chapters. Chap. 4 evi-
dences couplets of bicola constituting the acrostic units. Chap. 5
exhibits a single bicolon for each letter. Shea thereby identifies
a three-plus-two qīnāh meter in the total structure of the book.
The all-encompassing structural scheme of the book pulls the
individual threads together and exerts a centripetal force.

Gene M. Schramm ties the form and content together:

> If ever a case can be made for the symbolic nature of a
> particular poetic format, that of Lamentations is a prime
> example. The decline and fall of the alphabetic acrostic
> parallels the theme of this poem, the disintegration and
> vanishing of the kingdom of David and Solomon.[7]

## Association and Dissociation of Stanzas

A loose juxtaposition of heterogeneous parts is often a con-
comitant of acrostic patterning. Logical connections of the

lines according to generally accepted syntactic rules. He deviates from the stan-
dard only when he wishes to create a special effect." A hierarchy in the poetic line
thus emerges: meter, syntax, style ("The Qinah: A Study of Poetic Meter, Syntax
and Style," ZAW 95 [1983] 74).

[6] S. R. Driver, An Introduction to the Literature of the Old Testament (New York:
Charles Scribner's Sons, 1891) 420.

[7] G. M. Schramm, "Poetic Patterning in Biblical Hebrew" in Michigan Oriental
Studies in Honor of George C. Cameron, ed. L. L. Orlin (Ann Arbor: University of
Michigan, 1976) 178.

verses are often subordinate to the mechanical collocation of words beginning with the appropriate letter. In Lamentations the fragmenting, centrifugal nature of the verses does not become so diffuse as to destroy the unity. The poet balances the atomistic propensity of the alphabetic acrostic with a linking of the distinct letter stanzas into patterns. A variety of repetition schemes working throughout Lamentations effects a unity and coherence in the face of the threatening diffuseness.

The concatenation of stanzas in chap. 2, for example, reinforces the unity of the work in that chapter. In order that each lettered section articulate with its neighbor and not occur solely by virtue of the sequence of the alphabet, the poet reiterated in each verse a word or words appearing in the preceding verse. The following table, taken from Albert Condamin,[8] summarizes the concatenation:

| vv. 1-2 | 'dny | vv. 12-13 | none |
| vv. 2-3 | Y'qb | vv. 13-14 | apparent |
| vv. 3-4 | k'š | vv. 14-15 | |
| vv. 4-5 | k'yb | vv. 15-16 | 'lyk. . .šrqw |
| vv. 5-6 | šht | vv. 16-17 | 'lyk. . . 'wyb |
| vv. 6-7 | mw'd | vv. 17-18 | ywm |
| vv. 7-8 | hwmt | vv. 18-19 | lylh |
| vv. 8-9 | YHWH | vv. 19-20 | 'wllym |
| vv. 9-10 | 'rṣ | vv. 20-21 | hrq |
| vv. 10-11 | l'rṣ | vv. 21-22 | bywm 'p |
| vv. 11-12 | šfk, 'tp, brḥbt | | |

The general absence of logical development or narrative progress is a centrifugal factor impeding the coherence and simultaneity of the whole. The interlacing of verses with restated words contributes to the reading of the poem as a totality in terms of its dramatic wholeness.

The artistry of the poet is apparent in the careful balance achieved. Neither the loose nor the tight is permitted to preponderate. The artist simultaneously introduces associating centripetal elements, and develops atomistic, severing figures that tend away from integration. An elaborate tension between the contradictory tendencies is apparent in chap. 3. The threefold acrostic binds the discrete stanzas into a total set of twenty-two, i.e., the alphabetic totality, thus performing an integrating function. At the same time, the dividing of the total poem into discrete stanzas contributes to the opposite effect of

---

[8] A. Condamin, "Symmetrical Repetitions in *Lamentations* Chapters I and II," *JTS* 7 (1906) 140.

atomization. The poet develops this balance by strengthening and compacting each individual stanza to offset the unifying power of the ornate acrostic structure.

Within the three lines of each lettered stanza, the artist picks up and weaves a verbal root into the fabric of the stanza. This tightening of the structure of the individual stanza is accomplished at the expense of the cohesiveness of the whole poem. The individual lettered units rise in prominence and provide a counter-rhythm to the alphabetic integration into a totality. The following is a partial summary of this "intrastanza weave" in chap. 3:

|  |  |  |  |
|---|---|---|---|
| vv. 7 & 9 | qdr | vv. 31 & 33 | ky |
| v. 11 (bis) | drk | vv. 43 & 44 | skwth |
| v. 19 (bis) | zkwr | vv. 49 & 50 | 'yny |
| vv. 25 & 27 | ṭwb | vv. 59 & 60 | r'yth |

When the recurrences of analogous forms appear only within a single member, they function to set off that unit, tending away from the unity of the whole. But when the links occur between letter stanzas they exert a unifying force. The poet, however, does not let either tendency predominate.

The artist balances the work by crafting sections such as 3:18-20. The series of nine imperative verbs[9] in these three consecutive verses spanning three lettered stanzas of the alphabetic acrostic consolidates the work. Verbal and thematic links are also operative between the stanzas in chap. 3. These ties stand in contrast to the intrastanza weave described above.

## Shifts of Perspective

The changes of voices in Lamentations could have resulted in a fragmented kaleidoscopic effect. In the course of the short book, the poet uses no fewer than five personae which do not coincide with the five chapters of the work. The shifts in personae are abrupt; they occur with no explicit announcement or "stage direction." One persona is the representation of the city of Jerusalem as a woman brought to shame. What is more, this representation of the fallen woman vacillates between Jerusalem-as-city and Jerusalem-as woman! The poet's employment of the rhetorical device of adopting different masks runs the risk of "destroying the unity of the book, dissecting a totality into a se-

---

[9] If we accept the reading of Budde ṣa'ăqî for ṣā'aq, in light of the other two imperatives of v 18, we count 10 imperative verbs.

ries of discrete statements."[10] The threat of disunity is counter-
balanced, however, by the reader's deepened and broadened
grasp of the spiritual experience treated in the book. The ulti-
mate unity emerges as the reader realizes that the various per-
sonae are characterizations assumed by the poet as the medium
through which the artist perceives and expresses personal sor-
row. The subjective examinations complement the descriptions.
The final community prayer of chap. 5 is informed by all the
sufferers within the entire community. Just as the acrostic de-
vice suggests "totality" and "full range," so the five personae
suggest "*every* element and aspect of the *common* woe."[11]

A close study of the text reveals delicate external devices
that integrate the shifts of the speaker into the progression of
the work. Deliberate patterning is manifest in the relatively
even divisions in parts of the book. These divisions facilitate
seeing the text within a larger perspective. The delineations
help shape the mass of material. Chap. 1, comprised of 22
verses, falls into two equal parts marked by the shift in speaker.
Vv 1-11a, one half of the chapter, are written in the third person
about the reverses Jerusalem suffered. In the middle of v 11,
the city itself begins to speak. V 17 has the poet again speak but
v 18 reverts to the city expressing its own lament which contin-
ues to the end of the chapter. The poet employs formal integra-
tive elements to complement the thematic psychological
progression from the third person part to the first person
speech. Although the change of speaker lacks any explicit an-
nouncement, the short sudden emotional utterance in the first
person that intrudes itself in v 9c paves the way. V 9c is analo-
gous to the ejaculation in v 11c which introduces the shift.

v 9c    See, O YHWH, my misery, How the enemy jeers!
v 11c   See, O YHWH, and behold, How abject I have become!

The *NEB* is insensitive to the remote echoing and offers a
gratuitous levelling of the language in its translating vv 1-11
entirely in the third person. The distant paralleling of vv 9c and
11c anticipates and softens the change of speakers, preventing
disjuncture.

## Verbal Linking Amidst Shifts of Perspective

In chap. 2 there is also a shift in speaker. This change, too, is

[10] W. F. Lanahan, "The Speaking Voice in the Book of Lamentations," *JBL* 93
(1974) 41.
[11] Driver, *An Introduction*, 436.

not permitted to create compositional disunity. By placing the change in speaking voice at the very end of the chapter (vv 20-22 the poet brings the chapter to an intense climactic close.

> 2:20 See, O YHWH, and behold, to whom you have
> done this!
> Alas, women eat their own fruit, dandled babes.
> Alas, are slain in the Sanctuary of Lord, priest and
> prophet.
>
> 2:21 They lay on the ground in the streets young and
> old;
> My maidens and my youths fell by the sword.
> You slew [them] on your day of wrath; you
> slaughtered, you had no pity.
>
> 2:22 You summoned, as on a festival, my neighbors
> from round about;
> And there was not, on the day of YHWH's wrath,
> a survivor or remnant.
>
> Whom I dandled and multiplied, my enemy has
> annihilated.

In the course of chap. 2, the speaker reports on the Lord's destruction of Judah and His devastation of His city. So moved by the misery of the mother and children, the speaker abandons the reportage style in a poignant aside in v 11 (again, the precise central verse of the chapter).

> v 11 My eyes fail with tears;
> My bowels writhe [in anguish];
> My liver is poured on the earth.
> Over the ruin of the daughter of my people
> As children and infants languish in the streets of
> the city.

The reporter/poet shifts perspective from objective third person recorder of events until v 11, to subjective participant in the grief occasioned by those events. On one plane, the abrupt shift breaks the unity of the account, but, on a higher plane, the broadening of scope to include all involved, including witnesses, carries the theme further. On a subtle rhetorical level, the poet equates the witness and the victim. The distant echo of violated Jerusalem's moan in 1:20,

> Behold, O Lord, for I am in distress;
> My bowels writhe,
> My heart is turned within me.

is heard in the reporter's outcry in 2:11. This verbal linkage of the sorrow of victim and witness thematically strengthens the work as it formally integrates personae and chapters.

The poet suggests the immediate cause of the outcry in 2:11 by a verbal link centering on the repetition of the three letter stem *špk*, "pour, spill" in 2:11 and 2:12. The inter-verse tie tightens the structural and thematic composition of the work. "My liver is *poured out* on the earth" (2:11) is explained by "when they *pour out* their life at their mother's bosom" (2:12). The sight of the dying children makes it impossible for the poet/reporter to continue the cool recitation of calamities as done to this point. The poet now turns to the sufferers, to the city itself, in an extended apostrophe (vv 13-19). After rehearsing the devastation God visited upon Jerusalem, in v 18 the poet directs Zion to a cathartic mourning and consolation in the series of imperatives mentioned above. In vv 20-22 personified Zion addresses the Lord in another shift of speaker within the twenty-two verse chapter.

The final three verses of chap. 2 are held together by more than the common speaker. A grim play on words, and the related sounds of the labials "b" and "p," juxtaposes the women's dandling and pampering of their babies, *ōlĕlēy ṭippūḥum* (2:20) with the Lord's unmerciful slaughter of young and old, boy and girl, *ṭābaḥtā lō' ḥāmaltā* (2:21), and with the enemy's annihilation of those whom the mothers have dandled and multiplied *'ăšer ṭippaḥtī wĕribbītī*. Nor is that all! Vv 19 and 20 are further linked by the wordplay centered on the stem *'ll*:

v 19   . . .lift up your hands to Him for the life of your children (*ōlālayik*) . . .
v 20   See, O YHWH and behold to whom you have done this. . . . (*ōlaltā*) Alas women eat their own fruit, dandled babes . . . (*ōlĕlēy.*)

The sad association of the threatened lives of the children, the Lord's action and the cannibalized children are all three expressed by the same trilateral root (*'ll*). The grim pun ties the *qof* and *resh* letter stanzas together as it underscores the bleak theme.

With chap. 3 there is a striking case of a fourfold repetition of a key word. The word *geber*, "man" is the speaker who introduces himself in 3:1, "I am the man (*geber*) who has known affliction under the rod of His anger." The word *geber*, "man,"

is restated in vv 27, 35, and 39. The personal lament genre of
chap. 3 (similar to Ps 56) is signalled by this internal label
displayed within the work. The contents of chap. 3 set it apart
from the dirges sung by and for the city in chaps. 1, 2, and 4.
The individual male speaker, moreover, proclaims himself at
the outset and periodically recalls himself to the reader in the
course of the chapter. In very general, metaphoric terms, this
troubled man reviews the Lord's actions that have led to his
suffering. The first person outcries of pain alternate with a
description of the Lord's vehemence. V 22, precisely one-third
into the sixty-six-verse chapter, exhibits a turning point. It is
here that the laments change to expressions of hope and trust.
Externally, the poet signals the approaching shift to hope
through linkages of words with the same stem and with
synonymous words.

| | | |
|---|---|---|
| v 18 | I thought, my lasting *hope* in YHWH has perished | (*tōḥaltî*) |
| v 21 | therefore I have *hope* | (*'ōḥîl*) |
| v 24 | therefore I will *hope* | (*'ōḥîl*) |
| v 25 | YHWH is good to those who *trust* in Him | (*qōwāyw*) |
| v 26 | It is good that a man *hope* | (*yāḥîl*) |
| v 29 | There may yet be *hope* | (*tiqwāh*) |

The repetition of key words serves to communicate the
thematic reversals. The same words and their immediate
associations, uttered in different emotional states, poignantly
point up the psychic changes.

| | |
|---|---|
| v 17 | *My soul* despaired of peace *I forgot* everything *good* |
| v 20 | *My soul* surely *remembers* |
| v 24 | YHWH is my portion, My soul declares |
| v 25 | YHWH is *good* |

Delbert R. Hillers also identifies vv 17-21 as transitional,
from despair to hope.[12] The key he finds in v 18, "I thought, 'My
lasting hope in Yahweh has perished.' " On the basis of parallels
with other laments, Hillers writes that 3:18 "is already a hint
that a turning point is coming, because this sort of direct speech,
beginning, 'I thought (said). . .' is occasionally used in laments at
just such points" (cf. Jonah 2:5; Pss 31:22, 94:18, 139:11).[13] In

---

[12] D. R. Hillers, *Lamentations*, AB 7A (Garden City, N.Y.: Doubleday, 1979) 68.
[13] Ibid., 69.

addition to the verbal linkage between 3:18 and 3:21, the poet makes an explicit statement in 3:22 of the direct opposite of 3:18: "The kindness of YHWH has not ended, His mercies are not spent." The repeated words ease the transition of speaker and weave the discrete lines into a single structural entity and a thematic unity. The patterned shifts and the internal argument rescue the work from random piling up of verse upon verse.

Equal divisions with subtle markers also make for a cohesive text. In the chap. 3 acrostic, the *'aleph* to *zayin* stanzas, one-third of the twenty-two letter alphabet, are put in the mouth of a single sufferer who sinks to near total despair. At the one-third point, he remembers the kindness of YHWH and begins affirming His goodness. Another third of the alphabet marks off the expressions of trust uttered by the individual. The stanza beginning with the fourteenth letter of the Hebrew alphabet, *nun*, displays another shift of person. The individual gives way to the collective. Significantly, *nun* is the first person plural prefix and, beginning with this letter (v 4), the poet of Lamentations casts the lament in the plural and assumes the style of the national lament.[14] V 48 reverts again to the individual elegy. Thus, the central chapter of Lamentations closes with the same form with which it opened. Despite the changes of speakers, the balance is maintained by ancillary stabilizing factors at work which offset the potentially disruptive changes. These countervailing factors are the relatively even divisions of the text (as in the earlier chapters), and the appropriate junctures for these transitions that are subtly signalled.

Chap. 4 does not exhibit any abrupt shifts in speaker. The perspective of a single survivor is constant throughout.

In chap. 5, the first person singular persona is replaced by the communal "we." The style of chap. 5 is closest to that of the national lament and prayer, such as Pss 74 and 79. The collective perspective of chap. 5 is highlighted by the employment of similar sounds in relatively close juxtaposition. There are thirty-four instances within the twenty-two–verse chapter of the recurrence of the *-nū* suffix. This morpheme denotes the first person plural pronoun and serves as a *leitmotif* of the chapter. It ties together the distinct lines which do not have an acrostic bond (although the hint of the alphabetic whole in the number of verses is present). The restatement of *-nū*

---

[14] J. H. Tigay, "Lamentations, Book of," *EncJud* (Jerusalem: Keter Publishing House, 1972) 1372.

repeatedly tags the speaker(s) and underscores the collective theme. It also acts as a sort of rhyme which lends additional cohesiveness.

## Echoing and Verbal Links

The distant echo is also an effective means of linking and blending separate parts into a whole. Five times in chap. 1 the poet states "there is no one to comfort her" (1:2, 9, 16, 17, 21). This multiple reiteration emphasizes the important theme of isolation and helplessness. In a text in which the emotional pitch is rising, as is the case in chap. 1, each restatement recalls the earlier utterances and appears on a successively higher level of spiralling feeling. The earlier employments of the phrase infuse the final one with an added intensity. Generally, the Hebrew Bible prefers repetition with a variation to a verbatim restatement—the variation often revealing a subtle progress in the course of the text.[15] In chap. 1 the following variations on the theme of the absence of a comforter appear:

| | | |
|---|---|---|
| 1:2 | 'ēyn lāh měnaḥēm | There is not to her a comforter |
| 1:9 | 'eyn měnaḥēm lāh | There is no comforter to her |
| 1:16 | kī rāḥaq mimmennī měnaḥēm | For far from me is a[ny] comforter |
| 1:17 | 'ēyn měnaḥēm lāh | There is no comforter to her |
| 1:21 | 'ēyn měnaḥēm lī | There is no comforter to me |

Vv 2, 9 and 17 are virtually identical. There is but a slight transposition of subject and prepositional phrase in v 9 which carries no thematic signification. V 16 is the central occurrence of the theme and varies most from the others in form. V 21 is the final occurrence. In form it resembles vv 2, 9 and 17 with one significant climactic change. The first person is stressed by the prepositional phrase variation at the end of the line. The first person is further stressed by the word, 'ānī, "I," immediately preceding this phrase in v 21. The earlier apperances prepare the reader to expect "to her" to follow "there is no comforter." This expectation is artfully frustrated. Meaningfully, the isolation and misery of personified Jerusalem is expressed in the first person locution of the personified Jerusalem, "there is no comforter *to me*."

Remote echoing is noteworthy in 1:7 and 3:19. In each, a main theme is conveyed by the same three words:

[15] See D. Grossberg, "The Disparate Elements of the Inclusio in Psalms," *Hebrew Annual Review* 6 (1982) 97-104.

1:7   Jerusalem *remembered* her days of *affliction* and
      *misery*
3:19  to *remember* my *affliction* and *misery*

The poet achieves three important effects by employing the
same three words in the same sequence in 1:17 and 3:19. The
restatement focuses attention on the lines. The repetition also
emphasizes the major theme of Lamentations expressed in
these lines. The distant echo, furthermore, serves to link 1:7
and 3:19 and contributes too the compactness of the structure of
the work. It also contributes to the special texture of the work
just as the associative clusters in Song of Songs do for that work
*mutatis mutandis*.

## Thematic Ties

The single theme of grief at the fall of Jerusalem is the
strongest centripetal force of the book. Sorrow, the effect of the
destruction, is central and not the destruction itself. The all-per-
vasive emotional signature of the work compensates for the
centrifugal forces of shift of speakers and points of view. The
eyewitness reports interspersed with first person accounts by
personified Jerusalem, the communal prayer in the first person
plural, and the tale of personal suffering by a representative of
the people, each has its own literary characteristics. Neverthe-
less, the work does not fall apart; the constituent elements are
blended and the result is greater than the sum of the individual
parts. The multiple treatment of the same theme from differing
perspectives suggests that "no aspect of the common grief is un-
remembered. . .every trait which might stir a chord of sorrow or
regret is brought together for the purpose of completing the
picture of woe."[16] A constellation of centralizing devices com-
plements this thematic unity. The external and internal traits
alike integrate the parts into a totality.

## Degree of Historicity

In light of the fact that there is suppression of place, time
and order of events, the unity of the work is all the more re-
markable. The tension of the text, drawn together and pulled
apart, is in part a function of the degree of historicity within the
work. Facts and sequence contribute to a centripetally oriented
work. Ambiguity reduces textual coherence; interchangeable
parts lend a diffusion of content and direction.

---

[16] Driver, *An Introduction*, 430-31.

Lamentations lacks unifying factual details as does much lyrical poetry. A prose account of the fall of Jerusalem appears in 2 Kgs. This account is strikingly rich in names, places and dates. Lamentations achieves a cohesiveness despite its paucity of place names and personal names. The intention of the poet is not that of the prose writer. Historical details are not of the same import to both. Other than "Zion," the poet of Lamentations mentions very few place names. At the end of chap. 5 the poet does mention "Edom":

> Rejoice and be glad O daughter of Edom,. . .
> but to you also the cup shall pass;
> you shall become drunk and strip yourself bare
>
> . . .
>
> But your iniquity, O daughter of Edom, He will punish;
> He will uncover your sins. (4:21-22)

and in 5:6, Egypt and Assyria:

> We are hotly pursued.
> Exhausted, we are given no rest.
> We hold out a hand to Egypt;
> To Assyria, for our fill of bread.

Historical precision was not the aim in mentioning these specific proper names in these verses. The cry for vengeance on Edom is also found elsewhere in Hebrew poetry (Ps 137:7) and the reason for the curse against Edom is not given in Lamentations (cf. Obad 11-14 and Ezek 35). The imprecation is a tradition and convention rather than a factual datum. Egypt and Assyria are invoked in 5:6 as little more than a geographical merism, i.e., "east and west," to which the defeated Judeans might appeal for help. Assyria and Egypt are the two kingdoms that alternately rose to power in the ancient Near East. They are used here primarily as symbols and not as actual historical data. The absence of the real "names and dates" is a centrifugal aspect of the work.

### Radical and Traditional Imagery

Startling images and extraordinary figures focus attention on themselves at the expense of the total work, and they slow the reading. This is the case with many of the arresting images and abundant hyperbole in Song of Songs. The continuity of the Song is disturbed as the individual figure is pondered. The work is perceived as a string of gems in succession and not in its total fullness. Lamentations, too, exhibits striking tropes and gross exaggeration. These figures in Lamentations, however, are not permitted to cause disjuncture in the work. A peculiarity of the extravagant and hyperbolic imagery in Lamentations, in contrast to that of Song of Songs, is that the imagery in Lamentations is drawn from traditional literary locutions. The Lamentations figures have parallels elsewhere in Scripture. There are but sparse examples of affinities to the extravagant images of Song of Songs elsewhere in the Bible.

The effect of the recognition of inherited literary traditions in Lamentations anchors the work within a genre; it provides a key to its understanding and it accelerates the reading. Rather than arresting the progress, the conventional idiom tends toward the simultaneity of the work and curtails the excessive dwelling on the parts.

The phrase "daughter of X" appears extensively in Lamentations and in Jeremiah and also occurs in Micah and Isaiah. "My people," "Zion," "Judah," "Jerusalem" and "Edom" all appear as the variant second member of this phrase throughout Lamentations. Thus, we have: "daughters of my people," "daughter of Zion," "daughter of Judah," "daughter of Jerusalem" and daughter of Edom." The poetic effect is to dramatically express the metaphorical personification of the people, nation or city as a single woman. The frequency of the figure is a unifying element, a reprise, with centripetal force in Lamentations.

An aspect of the recurring personification of Zion and Jerusalem is the "widowed city" motif. This motif is not unique to Lam 1:1. It occurs also in Isa 47:8, 9; 54:4 and Jer 51:5. Chayim Cohen introduces a parallel from Egyptian literature as well.[17] His study of the biblical occurrences in light of the legal definition of Akkadian *almattu* in the Middle Assyrian Laws yields a fruitful understanding of this motif in the Bible. The nuance in the definition of *almattu* which provides a satisfactory interpretation for this motif is the special kind of widow—"a once married woman who has no means of financial support and who is thus in need of special legal protection."[18] When confronted first with the personification of the city as a woman and then as a widow the ancient reader/hearer grasped the metaphors immediately. They were part of the Israelite's cultural heritage and therefore did not retard the progress of the work.

Another item of literary tradition is the depiction of utmost

[17] C. Cohen, "The 'Widowed' City," *JANES* 5 (1973) 75-81.
[18] Ibid., 76.

hunger. The extremism of the siege and famine is stressed by the picture painted of mothers eating the fruit of their womb (vv 2:20 and 4:10). This grisly detail is not without parallel in Scripture. Regarding the siege of Samaria, 2 Kgs 6:28-30 relates a similar action. Hillers adduces numerous cases of cannibalism in the ancient Near East literary traditions, biblical and extrabiblical.[19] He concludes that in the poetry of Lamentations "the events are . . . refracted through an age-old tradition. In literature this [cannibalism] was how one stated that the utmost starvation had taken place."[20]

The poet in Lamentations invoked literary conventions to express the sorrow of Judah. These traditions were readily grasped by the audience who were able to assimilate them into the wholeness of the elegiac work.

> If the author of Lamentations says "For your ruin is as vast as the sea" [2:13] using a simile as old as Ugaritic literature, or can say that the iniquity of his people was greater than that of Sodom and Gomorrah [4:6], then we may suppose him capable of saying that the people turned cannibals, as a traditional and expressive way of depicting the severity of the suffering. From the religious side, this was a way of asserting that Yahweh had done what he threatened.[21]

A further figure of speech relating to the theme of desolation appears in 5:18. Mt. Zion lies desolate and foxes range over it. Although this is one of the few passages in Lamentations with mention of a place name, this verse should not be given historical credibility. The frequency of the phenomenon of wild animals prowling in the ruins (cf. Isa 34:11, 13; Isa 13:21-22) argues for a figurative meaning. One of the curses attached to the first Sefire treaty (Sef 1A 32-33) says,

> And may Arpad become a mound to (house the desert animal) and the gazelle and the fox and the hare and the wildcat and the owl and the (?) and the magpie.[22]

The ancient Israelite did not pause to ponder whether the wild creatures sought shelter in the rubble of the buildings, in the ruined basements or against the charred walls. He appreciated

---

[19] Hillers, "History and Poetry," *CurTM* 10 (1983) 155-61.
[20] Hillers, "History," 159.
[21] Ibid., 159-60.
[22] Quoted in Hillers, "History," 156.

the religious and emotional literary truth expressed and did not seek literal historical data. Jerusalem is suffering the *typical* fate of a wayward city.[23] It is described as ruined cities have been described within the literary tradition. The ties of an historical, objective referent to the images are lacking. Lamentations is dancing on the brink of incohesive expressionistic images, but does not stumble. The well-worn phrase, drawn from a common literary tradition, focuses and defines the poetic integrality.

The countervailing forces lending a dynamism to the work need to be borne in mind. The lack of historical, factual detail tends toward diffuseness. The employment of extreme and striking imagery supports the centrifugal leaning and threatens to break up the unity of the work. The traditional and conventional nature of the tropes balances the fragmenting pull. Although radical at first flush, the extremism of the figures abates as parallels are recalled which tie the trope to a particular type and thereby unify and merge the distinct and disparate into a common tradition.

## Closural Features

A weak ordering of elements and a tenuous goal-directed succession in Lamentations alternates with a tightness and integration produced by connective elements and features of closure. Lamentations owes its force to the precarious balance it strikes between openness and completeness, between process and finished object. Poetic closure is a major aspect of poetic form that fosters internal coherence as well as a sense of completeness.

The inclusio is a particular type of artistic restatement that provides a high degree of poetic closure. Chaps. 1 and 2 of Lamentations exhibit this device, providing a concentric framing design which tightens and fastens. The several symmetrically opposed stanzas of the opening chapter display repetitions of one or more words and resemble an extended chiasm. The restatements appear in the first and final stanzas (vv 1 and 22), the second and penultimate stanzas (vv 2 and 21), the third and third-from-last stanzas (v 3 and 20) and thus throughout, with but two pairs lacking an echo. Albert Condamin charted these repetitions in the following tables:[24]

---

[23] For some comparative material on the destruction of cities see J. Cooper, *The Curse of Agade* (Baltimore and London: Johns Hopkins University Press, 1983).
[24] Condamin, "Symmetrical," 139. Condamin also suggests a compelling transposition of verses which, if accepted, would complete the scheme.

CHAPTER 1

| | | | | |
|---|---|---|---|---|
| 1:1 | *rbty* | | 1:5 | *YHWH...hlkw šby* |
| 1:22 | *rbwt* | | 1:18 | *YHWH...hlkw bšby* |

The expression *hlk bšby* does not
occur elsewhere in this chap.

| | |
|---|---|
| 1:2 | *'yn ln mnḥm...l'ybym* |
| 1:21 | *'yn mnḥm lī...'yby* |

| | |
|---|---|
| 1:16 | *ṣywn* |
| 1:17 | *ṣywn* |

| | |
|---|---|
| 1:3 | *hmṣrym* |
| 1:20 | *ṣr* |

7-8 & 14-16
Emendation and transpotitions yield
repetitions in 7 & 14, 9 & 16. In 8 &
15 there is no important
correspondence.

| | |
|---|---|
| 1:4 | *khnyh* |
| 1:19 | *khny* |

The word *khn* occurs
nowhere else in this chap.

| | |
|---|---|
| 1:10 | *prś* |
| 1:13 | *prś* |

| | |
|---|---|
| 1:11 | *r'h...whbyṭ* |
| 1:12 | *hbyṭw wr'w* |

CHAPTER 2

| | | | | |
|---|---|---|---|---|
| 2:1 | *bywm 'pw* | | 2:7 | *'wyb...kywm* |
| 2:22 | *bywm 'p YHWH* | | 2:16 | *'wybyk...hywm* |

| | | | | |
|---|---|---|---|---|
| 2:2 | *l' ḥml...l'rṣ* | | 2:8 | *bt (ṣywn)* |
| 2:21 | *l'rṣ...l' ḥmlt* | | 2:15 | *bt (yrwšlm)* |

(No special significance is to be

| | | |
|---|---|---|
| 2:3 | *'klh* | attached to this repetition of *bt*, |
| 2:20 | *t'klnh* | which occurs in almost every section.) |

| | | | | |
|---|---|---|---|---|
| 2:4 | *špk* | | 2:9 | *nby'yh...ḥzwn* |
| 2:19 | *špky* | | 2:14 | *nby'yh...ḥzw* |

| | | | | |
|---|---|---|---|---|
| 2:5 | *'dny* | | 2:10 | *bt ṣywn...btwlt* |
| 2:18 | *'dny* | | 2:13 | *btwlt bt ṣywn* |

| | | | | |
|---|---|---|---|---|
| 2:6 | *YHWH* | | 2:11 | *nšpk...b'ṭp...brḥwbwt* |
| 2:17 | *YHWH* | | 2:12 | *bht'ṭpm...brḥwbwt...bḥšṭpk* |

Such an extensive chiastic pattern creates a compactness in the
two chapters that creates and reinforces a strong closure.

An artist attempts proper closure in order to reinforce the
finality, autonomy and resolution of the work. On a formal level
the shift of the final member signals the conclusion. This
principle of terminal modification is employed in Lamentations.
Chap. 5 does not have the explicit alphabetic acrostic structure
common to chaps. 1-4. Chap. 5 is also the shortest. Chap. 5 also

lacks the *qīnāh* rhythm. Moreover, it is chap. 5 that is fully a prayer to YHWH written entirely in the first person plural. In some traditions chap. 5 is also provided with the title, "A Prayer of Jeremiah." In each of the above, chap. 5 varies from the patterns established in the preceding chapters. The structural and content differences exploit the well-attested technique of terminal variation providing striking closure.[25]

The possible interpretation of Lamentations as an arbitrary, whimsical conglomeration of styles is disqualified in favor of the view of a deliberate, compositional design. Not solely by virtue of its divergence from the style of chaps. 1-4 does the final chapter provide fitting closure. This codalike chapter recapitulates the motifs of the entire work in a less elaborated form and serves as the concluding prayer of the entire work. The voice of chap. 5 is well described by W. F. Lanahan as "a choral voice. . . subsuming each individual persona [appearing in chaps. 1-4] in an act of prayer."[26]

Chap. 5 on the one hand differs greatly from 1-4—providing an obvious centrifugal drive. The drive is checked by the recognition that the differences constitute terminal modification. The several variations in this final member demand further compensatory centripetal forces, however, to cement the work. Without these balancing features, the variations would not be construed as completing the poem but as atomizing the parts. In addition to the common theme of all five chapters, the twenty-two line poem of chap. 5 coheres with the twenty-two letter alphabetic acrostics that precede it and thus serve to hold the work together.

Michael S. Moore identified in chap. 5 references to the many human groupings evoked earlier in the book.

| | | |
|---|---|---|
| a) orphans (5:3) | e) virgins (5:11) | i) young boys (5:13) |
| b) mothers (5:3) | f) princes (5:12) | j) old men (5:14) |
| c) fathers (5:7) | g) elders (5:12) | k) young men (5:14)[27] |
| d) women (5:11) | h) youths (5:13) | |

Chap. 5 picks up the threads of the very broad array of suffering humanity woven into the tapestry of the work. This closural coda functions to prevent the formally distinct chapter from destroying the unity of the whole.

[25] Cf. Prov 31:10-31. The final section of Proverbs, a hymn in an alphabetic acrostic style differing structurally from the entire book of Proverbs, is an analogous manifestation of terminal modification. See also Ps 119 and Ps 134.

[26] Lanahan, "The Speaking Voice," 48.

[27] M. S. Moore, "Human Suffering in Lamentations," *RB* (1983) 552.

*Prayer as Generic Closure*

As one recognizes particular genre features in a work, one is better able to type the work and anticipate its compositional elements. These elements exert an influence on the reader's expectations regarding the development, structure and conclusion of the text. Thus "set up," the reader experiences the simultaneity of the text. The unprepared reader, conversely, experiences the text only as a loose succession of individual features unfolding seriatim.

The artist of Lamentations creates the work within the generic conventions of the elegy. The tradition of ending a national or individual lament, funeral dirge or other composition of grief on a note of prayer for God's intervention is to be found in the laments in Pss 28:9, 44:27, 74:18-23, and 86:16-17. It is also common to each chapter of Lamentations. The entreaty is often couched in the precative perfect, defined by Mitchell Dahood as "a verb form, often balanced by an imperative, that states an ardent wish or prayer."[28] Chap. 1 exhibits a turning to the Lord in vv 20-22 which represents an emotional and psychological release in an appeal to God to see the grief, hear the groan[29] and bring forth retribution against the enemy.

Chap. 2 comes to a close on a prayer-type utterance reminiscent of chap. 1, although there is no specific appeal to the Lord for vengeance. Lam 2:20 begins, "See, O Lord, and behold."

Chap. 3 exhibits a final section marked by direct address to YHWH. Lam 3:55-59 is an appeal to YHWH to show mercy to the soul in distress. The verbal form employed is the precative perfect. V 60 continues the apostrophe to the Lord importuning His retributive action against the jeering assailants.

Chap. 4 ends on a seeking of God's aid, too. The sorry state of Judah is the subject of vv 1-20. V 21 introduces a curse uttered against Edom.

Robert Gordis interprets the closing verse of Lamentations as "crucial for the meaning and spirit of the entire poem."[30] Understood in this way, Lam 5:21-22 present appropriate closure to the prayer of the final chapter and to the whole book. The common renderings of the last verse of chap. 5, however, either take undue liberties with the MT or do not appear appropriate for the close of a prayer.

---

[28] Dahood, *Psalms II*, AB 17 (Garden City, N.Y.: Doubleday, 1968) xi.

[29] Repointing *šāmĕ'ū* as imperative seems justified in light of the imperative *rĕ'ēh*, "see!" and the precative perfect *hēbē'tā*, "bring forth" in vv 20-21.

[30] R. Gordis, "The Conclusion of the Book of Lamentations 5:22," *JBL* 93 (1974) 289.

*NEB*  O lord, turn us back to thyself and we will come
       back;
       renew our days as in times long past.
       For if thou hast utterly rejected us,
       then great indeed has been thy anger against us.

*RSV*  Restore us to thyself, O Lord, that we may be
       restored!
       Renew our days as of old!
       Or hast thou utterly rejected us?
       Art though exceedingly angry with us?

*NJPS* Take us back, O Lord, to Yourself,
       And let us come back;
       Renew our days as of old!
       For truly, you have rejected us,
       Bitterly raged against us.

*JPSV* Turn Thou us unto Thee, O Lord, and we shall be
       turned; Renew our days as of old.
       Thou canst not have utterly rejected us
       And be exceeding wroth against us!

*AB*   bring us back to you, Yahweh, and we will return.
       Make our days as they were before.
       But instead you have completely rejected us;
       You have been very angry with us.

Each of the translations cited understands 5:21 as constituting a
plea. Gordis proposes that 5:22 c and d present the support for
the petition; he translates the cola in the following way. Note
the verb tenses:

> . . .you had despised us greatly
> and were very angry with us (5:22 c and d)

The plea and the foundation for the plea are conjoined by *kī 'im*
which Gordis renders "even if, even though, although." He ba-
ses his construal of this conjunction on Jer 51:14; Isa 10:22, Amos
5:22 and Lam 3:32. Gordis further points to Ps 89:51-52 as ex-
hibiting the same syntactic structure as Lam 5:21-22: ". . . a plea
extending over two verses, the petition being expressed by a
main clause containing the petition, (Ps 89:15), while the sup-
porting grounds or circumstances are presented in a following
subordinate clause (89:52)."[31] Thus, we have a fitting conclusion
for the work. The predominant wailful lament of chaps. 1-5 is
the reaction to the Lord's anger and spurning. Lam 5:22 alludes
to the Lord's rage and rebuff as now coming to an end. Despite

[31] Gordis, "The Conclusion," 291.

the Lord's prior fury the petitioner entreats him to turn back time to be like the pre-wrathful era.

There is a final, noteworthy, combined form/content element leading to a satisfying sense of closure at the end of the complete book. The particular language of the final plea to the Lord (5:21) contains the terms "bring us back," "we will return" and "as of old." These phrases suggest a completion and a look towards a return to the halcyon days. The poet conveys in these words the feeling of having gone full term and full circuit. Are not the longed for "days of old" of the final plea of the book (5:22) the days when Jerusalem was "full of people," "greatest among nations," and "the noblest of the states" of the opening of the book (1:1)? This figure is akin to the inclusio; it is a return to the point at which the reader began. The poet does not, however, employ the same phrase or sentence at the beginning and end of the work. The trope here is more of a closural allusion that fits well into the poem's thematic structure.

# CONCLUSION

I have focused my attention on the poetic structure of Songs of Ascents, Song of Songs, and Lamentations, describing the overall configuration of each from a new perspective. I provide a reading that seriously addresses the whole of the relevant texts and not just individual parts like word-pairs or poetic lines. I have also analyzed features in the poems which have more than one function. Numerous compositional features are at work in each text within and above the level of the individual sentence. I have identified and discussed features from the phonological realm, the lexical field, the grammatical domain, including morphology and syntax, and the semantic sphere embracing imagery, narrative development and theme. All these features interact dynamically within the poems, creating an artistic tension and characterizing the totality of each of the poems differently. The ancient Hebrew poets employed the structural features deliberately and carefully striking a delicate balance along the structural continuum between the centripetal and centrifugal extremes. The centripetal extreme features the whole; the centrifugal highlights the parts.

The concerted work of the many compositional features of Songs of Ascents, Song of Songs and Lamentations illuminates the relationships obtaining among form, function and content of each. This investigation provides a register of characteristics of compositional forms effective in treating other poetic works as well. The catalogue further proves helpful in addressing the crux, "What is biblical poetry?" Centripetal and centrifugal forces emerge as significant categories in the study of biblical poetic composition.

# BIBLIOGRAPHY

Aletti, Jean-Noël and Trublet, Jacques. *Approche poétique et théologique des psaumes*. Paris: Initiation, Editions du Cerf, 1983.

Alonso-Schökel, Luis. *Treinta salmos: poesía y oración*. Estudios de Antiguo Testamento 2. Madrid: Ediciones Cristiandad, 1981.

Alter, Robert. *The Art of Biblical Poetry*. New York: Basic Books, 1985.

Alter, Robert. "Introduction to the Old Testament." In *The Literary Guide to the Bible*, edited by Robert Alter and Frank Kermode. Cambridge: The Belknap Press of Harvard University Press, 1987.

Angénieux, J. "Structure du Cantique des Cantique." *ETL* 96-142.

Angénieux, J. "Les trois portraits du Cantique des Cantiques." *ETL* 42 (1966) 582-96.

Angénieux, J. "Le Cantique des Cantiques en huit chants à refrains alternants." *ETL* 44 (1968) 87-140.

Armfield, H. T. *The Gradual Psalms: A Treatise on the Fifteen Songs of Degrees with Commentary*. London: J. T. Hayes, 1874.

Baker, Joshua and Nicholson, Ernest W. *The Commentary of Rabbi David Kimḥe on Psalms cxx-cl*. Cambridge: At the University Press, 1973.

Beaucamp, Evode. "L'unité du Recueil des Montées: Psaumes 120-134." *Liber annus Studium Biblicum Franciscanum* 29 (1979) 73-90.

Berlin, Adele "Motif and Creativity in Biblical Poetry." *Prooftexts* 3 (1983) 231-41.

Berlin, Adele. *The Dynamics of Biblical Parallelism*. Bloomington: Indiana University Press, 1985.

Bloom, Edward A., Philbrick, Charles H. and Blistein, Elmer, M. *The Order of Poetry: An Introduction*. New York: Odyssey Press, 1961.

Bovet, Felix. *Les Psaumes des Maalaoth*. Paris: Neuchatel, 1889.

Broadribb, Donald. "A Historical Review of Studies of Hebrew Poetry." *Abr-N* 13 (1972) 66-87.

Brooks, Cleanth. *The Well Wrought Urn, Studies in the Structure of Poetry.* New York: Harcourt, Brace and Company, 1947.

Budde, K. "Das hebräische Klagelied." *ZAW* 2 (1882) 1-52.

Burke, Kenneth. *Counter-Statement.* Berkeley: University of California Press, 1968.

Buzy, T. R. D. "La composition littéraire du Cantique des Cantiques." *RB* 49 (1940) 169-94.

Cohen, Chayim. "The 'Widowed' City." *JANES* 5 (1973) 75-81.

Cohen, Chayim. "Studies in Early Israelite Poetry I: An Unrecognized Case of Three-Line Staircase Parallelism in the Song of the Sea." *JANES* 7 (1975) 13-17.

Condamin, Albert. "Symmetrical Repetitions in *Lamentations* Chapter I and II." *JTS* 7 (1906) 137-40.

Cooper, Jerrold S. *The Curse of Agade.* Baltimore and London: Johns Hopkins University Press, 1983.

Dahood, Mitchell. *Psalms II.* AB 17. Garden City, N.Y.: Doubleday, 1968.

Dahood, Mitchell. *Psalms III.* AB 17A Garden City, N.Y.: Doubleday, 1970.

Driver, G. R. "Supposed Arabisms in the Old Testament." *JBL* 55 (1936) 101-20.

Driver, S. R. *An Introduction of the Literature of the Old Testament.* New York: Charles Scribner's Sons, 1891.

Exum, J. Cheryl. "A Literary and Structural Analysis of the Songs of Songs." *ZAW* 85 (1973) 47-79.

Fisch, Harold. *Poetry With A Purpose: Biblical Poetics and Interpretation.* Bloomington: Indiana University Press, 1988.

Fox, Michael V. *The Song of Songs and the Ancient Egyptian Love Songs.* Madison and London: University of Wisconsin Press, 1985.

Garr, W. Randall, "The Qinah: A Study of Poetic Meter, Syntax, and Style." *ZAW* 95 (1983) 54-75.

Gordis, Robert. "The Conclusion of the Book of Lamentations 5:22." *JBL* 93 (1974) 289-93.

Gordis, Robert. *The Song of Songs and Lamentations: A Study, Modern Translation and Commentary.* Rev. and aug. ed. New York: KTAV, 1974.

Gordon, Cyrus H. "New Light on the Hebrew Language." *Hebrew Abstracts: A Journal of Hebraic, Biblical and Related Studies* 15 (1974) 29-31.

Gordon, Cyrus H. "New Directions." *BASP* 15 (1978) 59-66.

Greenstein, Edward L. "Two Variations of Grammatical Parallelism in Canaanite Poetry and Their Psycholinguistic Background." *JANES* 6 (1974) 87-105.

Grossberg, Daniel. "Noun/Verb Parallelism: Syntactic or Asyntactic." *JBL* 99 (1980) 481-88.

Grossberg, Daniel, "The Disparate Elements of the Inclusio in Psalms," *Hebrew Annual Review* 6 (1982) 97-104.

Grossberg, Daniel. "A Centrifugal Structure in Biblical Poetry." *Semiotica* 58 (1986) 139-150.

Gunkel, Hermann. *Einleitung in die Psalmen.* Göttingen: Vandenhoeck und Ruprecht, 1933.

Gutwinski, Waldemar. *Cohesion in Literary Texts: A Study of Some Grammatical and Lexical Features of English Discourse.* The Hague and Paris: Mouton, 1976.

Halliday, M. A. K. and Hasan, Ruquaiya. *Cohesion in English* (London: Longman, 1976.

Hillers, Delbert R. *Lamentations.* AB 7A. Garden City, N.Y.: Doubleday, 1972.

Hillers, Delbert R. "History and Poetry." *CurTM* 10 (1983) 155-61.

Homerus. *The Odyssey of Homer,* translated by R. A. Lattimore. New York: Harper and Row, 1967.

Hopkins, Gerard Manley. "On the Origins of Beauty." In *The Journals and Papers,* edited by H. House. New York and Toronto: Oxford University Press, 1959.

Jakobson, Roman. "Linguistics and Poetics." In *Style in Language,* edited by T. Sebeok. Cambridge: MIT Press, 1960.

Keet, Cuthbert C. *A Study of the Psalms of Ascents: A Critical and Exegetical Commentary upon Psalms cxx-cxxxiv.* London: Mitre Press, 1969.

Kittel, Rudolf. *Die Psalmen übersetzt und erklart.* Leipzig, 1929.

Kugel, James L. *The Idea of Biblical Poetry, Parallelism and Its History.* New Haven and London: Yale University Press, 1981.

Lanahan, William F. "The Speaking Voice in the Book of Lamentations." *JBL* 93 (1974) 41-49.

Landy, Francis. *Paradoxes of Paradise: Identity and Difference in the Song of Songs.* Sheffield: Almond Press, 1983.

Liebreich, Leon J. "The Songs of Ascents and the Priestly Blessing." *JBL* 74 (1955) 33-36.

Mannati, Marina. "Les psaumes graduels constituent-ils un

genre littéraire distinct à l'intérieur du psautier biblique?" *Sem* 29 (1979) 85-100.

Meek, Theophile J. "The Song of Songs: Introduction and Exegesis." *IB* 5 New York and Nashville: Abingdon Press, 1956.

Mintz, Alan. "The Rhetoric of Lamentations and the Representation of Catastrophe." *Prooftexts* 2 (1982) 1-17.

Mintz, Alan. *Ḥurban: Responses to Catastrophe in Hebrew Literature.* New York: Columbia University Press, 1984.

*The Mishnah translated from the Hebrew with Introduction and Brief Explanatory Notes* by Herbert Danby. London: Oxford University Press, 1933.

Mizener, Arthur. "The Romanticism of W. B. Yeats." *The Southern Review* 7 (1942) 601-23.

Moore, Michael S. "Human Suffering in Lamentations." *RB* 90 (1983) 534-55.

Murphy, Roland E. "Canticle of Canticles." *JBC*, edited by R. E. Brown, J. A. Fitzmyer and R. E. Murphy. Englewood Cliffs, N.J.: Prentice Hall, 1968.

Murphy, Roland E. "The Unity of the Song of Songs." *VT* 29 (1979) 436-43.

Neale, J. M. and Littledale, R. F. *A Commentary on the Psalms from Primitive and Medieval Writers.* London: Joseph Masters & Co., 1883.

Pope, Marvin H. *Song of Songs.* AB 7C (Garden City, N.Y.: Doubleday, 1977.

Pouguet, W. and Guitton, J. *The Canticle of Canticles.* New York: Declan X. McMullen, 1948.

Rendsburg, Gary A. "Janus Parallelism in Gen 49:26." *JBL* 99 (1980) 291-93.

Robinson, Theodore M. *The Poetry of the Old Testament.* London: Gerald Duckworth and Co., 1947.

Sandmel, Samuel. *The Hebrew Scriptures: An Introduction to their Literature and Religious Ideas.* New York: Oxford University Press, 1963.

Sawyer, John F. A. "An Analysis of the Context and Meaning of the Psalm-Headings." *Transactions of the Glasgow University Oriental Society* 22 (1967-68) 26-38.

Schramm, Gene M. "Poetic Patterning in Biblical Hebrew." In *Michigan Oriental Studies in honor of George G. Cameron*, edited by Louis L. Orlin. Ann Arbor: University of Michigan, 1976.

Shea, William H. "The *qînāh* Structure of the Book of Lamentations." *Bib* 60 (1979) 103-7.

Shea, William. "The Chiastic Structure of the Song of Songs." *ZAW* 92 (1980) 378-96.

Stankiewicz, Edward. "Centripetal and Centrifugal Structures in Poetry." *Semiotica* 38 (1982) 217-42.

Taylor, William R. and McCullough, W. Stewart. "Psalms: Introduction and Exegesis." *IB*. New York: Abingdon Press, 1955.

Thilo, M. *Das Hohelied neu übersetzt und ästhetischesittlich beurteilt*. Bonn: A. Marcus and E. Weber, 1921.

Tigay, Jeffrey H. "Lamentations, Book of." *EncJud*. Jerusalem: Keter Publishing House, 1972.

Waterman, L. *The Song of Songs Translated and Interpreted as a Dramatic Poem*. Ann Arbor: University of Michigan Press, 1948.

Watson, Wilfred G. E. *Classical Hebrew Poetry: A Guide to its Techniques*. JSOTSup 26. Sheffield: JSOT Press, 1984.

Weiser, Artur. *The Psalms: A Commentary*. Philadelphia: Westminster Press, 1962.

Wells, Henry W. *Poetic Imagery*. New York: Russel and Russel, 1961.

Wilson, Gerald Henry, *The Editing of the Hebrew Psalter*. SBLDS 76. Chico, Calif.: Scholars Press, 1985.

## DATE DUE